LITURGY/VOL. 2

# CONCILIUM

THEOLOGY IN THE AGE OF RENEWAL

# CONCILIUM

# LITURGY / VOL. 2

# THE
# CHURCH
## AND THE
# LITURGY

# LITURGY VOL. 2

*CONCILIUM*
*theology in the age*
*of renewal*

PAULIST PRESS/GLEN ROCK, NEW JERSEY

NIHIL OBSTAT: James F. Rigney, S.T.D.
*Censor Librorum*

IMPRIMATUR: ✠ Francis Cardinal Spellman
*Archbishop of New York*

December 31, 1964

Library of Congress Catalogue Card Number: 65-17869

English Translation © 1965 by
*Paulist Fathers, Inc.* and *Stichting Concilium*

BOOK DESIGN: Claude Ponsot

PAULIST PRESS
EXECUTIVE OFFICES: 21 Harristown Road, Glen Rock, New Jersey
*Executive Publisher:* John A. Carr, C.S.P.
*Executive Manager:* Alvin A. Illig, C.S.P.
*Asst. Executive Manager:* Thomas E. Comber, C.S.P.

EDITORIAL OFFICES: 304 W. 58th Street, New York, N.Y.
*Editor:* Kevin A. Lynch, C.S.P.
*Managing Editor:* Urban P. Intondi

Manufactured in the United States of America

# CONTENTS

# PART II

## BIBLIOGRAPHICAL SURVEY

# PART III

## DO-C: DOCUMENTATION CONCILIUM

# PART IV

## CHRONICLE OF THE LIVING CHURCH

# *PREFACE*

Johannes Wagner/*Trier, W. Germany*

Histtory tells of frequent liturgical reforms, for the liturgy of the Church is not only the work of God but also of men. Thus, it is subject to the law of aging and is in need of constant renewal. However, the phenomenon of a movement of general ecclesiastical renewal carried on in the name of the liturgy, drawing its strength from the act of public worship and making the renewal of this worship its main purpose, is something new in history.

No matter how we date the beginning of this phenomenon: whether it be the "Event of Malines" of September 23, 1909, or the encyclical *Tra le sollecitudini* of Pope St. Pius X on November 22, 1903, or the romantic undertaking of the Benedictine Abbot Guéranger and his foundation of Solesmes in 1833, or again, the periodic change in spirituality as a whole, as happened with the liturgical aims of moderate enlightenment at the beginning of the 19th century but to some extent already in the 18th, or a number of even earlier yet always interrupted attempts —in every case it is easy to see that the "pastoral" element was quite consciously present.

1

It was never a question of liturgy for liturgy's sake; never a mere rational reform of the liturgy for the sake of greater intelligibility; never an antiquarian hankering after ancient forms; never a mere aesthetic effort in the sense of "art for art's sake"; rather, it always had a commitment of its own. There was always a concern with the various ways in which religious realities are experienced in the liturgy, and with the conviction that men could be brought in contact with these realities through this liturgy. The liturgical movement had from its very start and by intent a pastoral purpose, although to a different degree, in different ways and with different emphasis in its various phases.

In the course of its variegated history this no longer young movement has become more aware of its true nature. It has become clear that the word "pastoral" does not adequately express its real nature unless one understands this word in a much deeper and more comprehensive sense than just one method among others such as, *e.g.,* pastoral care through liturgy or starting from the altar or the like. All these conceptions are insufficient. In the liturgical movement something is coming to the fore which is deeper and underlies all pastoral activity as its very foundation.

The new basis of pastoral work is seen in the emergence of a new consciousness of the Church. The Church awakens in the souls (Guardini). The People of God becomes conscious of itself in divine worship. The liturgical celebration is the holy gathering of the People of God. In this gathering the People becomes visible as a whole and in its different states that are neither interchangeable nor replaceable. They are hierarchically distinct and yet ordered toward one another, each operative in its own way and constituting the whole only by their cooperation. In liturgical worship, the Church becomes an "event" (Rahner). In it and through it, here and now, the gathering of "those called out" to be the *ecclesia* takes place; there takes place the sacred *commercium* of God with his chosen people: the Lord is in the midst of the gathering of his own. In fact, this gathering becomes holy only by his presence in their midst. He gives himself to his own while they answer with thanksgiving and praise.

The liturgical movement, which has brought about a new awareness of all this, is ultimately but a part, the specific expression and an important interpretation of a much greater and more comprehensive process that has been going on in the Church irresistibly for a long time: the image of the Church is seen in a new light; it is seen and made a reality in a new and more profound manner.

Thus, it should not be considered a mere accident or, worse, a way out of an embarrassment that Vatican Council II, whose special purpose according to Pope Paul VI is a deeper and more comprehensive self-awareness of the Church, devoted so much time to the discussion of divine worship and approved the Constitution on the Sacred Liturgy as the first fruit of its labor. With the discussion of the schema on the liturgy the Council was from the first day dealing with its proper object: *De Ecclesia*. To many, God's Plan thus appears much more clearly. The words of Pope Pius XII calling the liturgical movement a passing of the Holy Spirit through the Church is confirmed once more.

The Constitution on the Sacred Liturgy of Vatican Council II is a document that deserves the special attention of every member of the Church. Not only the concrete norms of the liturgical reform should be studied but especially the ecclesial character of its theological declarations and general directions. Finally, close consideration should also be given to the ecclesial import of those principles—some of them not even formally stated—since they inspire and harmoniously integrate other norms and directions.

The second volume of CONCILIUM is devoted to the Constitution on the Sacred Liturgy of Vatican Council II. It seemed, then, imperative to put some of the ecclesial aspects of this Constitution in focus.

# PART I

## ARTICLES

# CIPRIANO VAGAGGINI, O.S.B.

Born October 3, 1909 in Piancastagnaio, Italy.
He became a Benedictine and was ordained July
30, 1934. He studied at the Collegio di Sant'
Anselmo in Rome, the University of Louvain in
Belgium and the Pontifical Oriental Institute,
Rome. He earned his doctorate in philosophy in
1932 with the thesis, "Il aspetto metafisico del
concetto del bello"; his doctorate in theology in
1937 with the thesis, "Maria nelle opere di Ori-
gene"; his doctorate in ecclesiastical oriental sciences in 1940 with the book, *I Patriarchi orientali
cattolici*. From 1942 to 1962 he was professor
of dogmatic theology at the Collegio di Sant'
Anselmo in Rome. He is a *peritus* of Vatican
Council II, and a consultor in drawing up the
Constitution on the Sacred Liturgy.

Cipriano Vagaggini, O.S.B. / *Bologna, Italy*

# The Bishop
# and the Liturgy

The purpose of this article is to illustrate the theological bases upon which, according to the Constitution on the Sacred Liturgy of Vatican Council II, the full range of bishop-liturgy relationships rests.

These bases are very clearly set forth at various places in the Constitution. In my opinion, one need only point out and illustrate them within the limits of the Council's ecclesiology.

The Council's basic statement on the matter is contained in article 41 that deals with the liturgical life of the dioceses:

> The bishop is to be considered as the high priest of his flock, from whom the life in Christ of his faithful is in some way derived and dependent.
>
> Therefore all should hold in great esteem the liturgical life of the diocese centered around the bishop, especially in his cathedral church; they must be convinced that the preeminent manifestation of the Church consists in the full active participation of all God's holy People in these liturgical celebrations, especially in the same eucharist, in a single

prayer, at one altar, at which there presides the bishop surrounded by his college of priests and by his ministers.

Thus, the bishop considered chiefly as the high priest of his
flock (we shall see later that this is the real meaning of the Constitution), and the Church seen as realizing and manifesting itself
principally through the liturgical celebrations (above all, that of
the eucharist) with full participation of all the people around the
bishop—these are the two concepts that must be explained, first
of all, in the immediate and general context of the Council.

I

### The Bishop within the Pyramid of the Church, Seen from Its Base

The first perspective that helps one grasp the meaning of the
preceding statements is a certain way of viewing the Church as
the union of the dispersed children of God. Even though sinners,
they are his rightful possession; hence he, in his desire to make
them his own People, unites and orders them under their
bishops. Thus they stand united to himself and among themselves in partaking of divine life. This concept is explicitly contained in article 26 of the Constitution:

> Liturgical services are not private functions, but are cele-
> brations of the Church, which is the "sacrament of unity",
> namely, the holy People united and ordered under their
> bishops.

The terminology is taken from St. Cyprian. The Church is
*unitatis sacramentum*[1] because it is cause, expression and symbol of the unity of men with God and among themselves through
their sharing in the unity of the Father, the Son and the Holy
Spirit.[2] Therefore, the Church can be defined as *de unitate Pa-
tris et Filii et Spiritus Sancti plebs adunata*.[3]

---

[1] St. Cyprian, *De Cath. Eccl. Unitate*, 7.
[2] *Ibid.*, 6.
[3] St. Cyprian, *De Dom. Oratione*, 23.

In this unity, the bishop is the external and immediate principle of cohesion; the Church is the *plebs sancta sacerdoti* (read *episcopo*) *adunata et pastori suo grex adhaerens.*[4] Therefore, either a Church without her legitimate bishop or a bishop outside the bounds of the Church, is inconceivable *unde scire debes episcopum in Ecclesia esse et Ecclesiam in episcopo.*[5]

The universal Church is formed of the union of the local Churches in virtue of the communion of bishops among themselves and of the resulting unity: . . . *quando Ecclesia quae catholica una est scissa non sit neque divisa, sed utique connexa et cohaerentium sibi invicem sacerdotum glutino copulata.*[6] This conception of the Church is perfectly orthodox. However, for it to be complete also in its expression of revealed truth, especially in view of the known proclamation of the doctrine of the primacy of the Roman pontiff, it suffices to add (more expressly than St. Cyprian does) that communion with the pope is the non-replaceable principle, willed by God, of the unity of the single bishops and of the faithful in the universal Church. Hence it is the principle of their being true pastors and unifiers of the holy People participating in the unity of the Father, the Son and the Holy Spirit. And it is as a realization of this principle that the pope, in safeguarding the common good of this unity, has also the power to curb the bishop in the exercise of his authority, even though the same was fully and directly received by him from God on being consecrated a bishop to lead the flock entrusted to him on the way to salvation.

It is all a way of viewing the structure of the Church as a pyramid, so to speak, starting with the base: the children of God, separated from him and among themselves and scattered through the world because of sin, are reunited and restored to the status of holy People by virtue of their participation in the unity of the Father, the Son and the Holy Spirit. To that end, God chooses, from among the faithful themselves, some—

[4] Ep. 66,8.
[5] *Ibid.*
[6] *Ibid.*

the bishops—to serve and to become the driving force of reunification in the communion of supernatural life; he also invests them with the full powers necessary for the fulfillment of their task. But in order to preserve the universal unity and that cohesion itself, which is the very essence of the Catholic Church, outside of which there is no salvation, he designates one among the pastors and confers on him the powers necessary to perform his universal mission, including the authority to limit, for the common good, the exercise of powers that are *per se* connatural to each individual bishop.

This view, briefly outlined in the Constitution on the Sacred Liturgy, is the well-known basis for the whole vision of the Church in the Constitution *De Ecclesia* of Vatican Council II. It is dealt with at length in the opening chapters.

This view, somehow, is in contrast with the position taken by a certain school of ecclesiologists, reflected in the manuals of the time after Vatican Council I.

In these the whole body of the Church was often presented in such a way that the pope alone seemed to receive full light while the other components seemed to live by mere reflection. As a result, the whole construction seemed to derive its structural strength from that very light, the pope, subjecting the viewer to the optical illusion that the Church was nothing but a hierarchy of which the *plebs Dei* was a mere appendix, or, at best, the object and not the subject of power. This inevitably led one to conclude that all powers stemmed directly from the pope and that the function of the bishop was a mere vicarship.

Why had the Constitution on the Sacred Liturgy instinctively taken an opposite position, beginning with the *plebs Dei* and the bishops, even before the matter had come up for discussion in the Council? (It is known, in fact, that the first draft of the *De Ecclesia* mirrored quite closely the ecclesiological views mentioned above.) Because only within this perspective is it possible to value and understand (1) the doctrine by which the hierarchy and its powers, although derived from God and not from the people, are at the service of the *plebs Dei;* (2) the doctrine of the universal priesthood of the faithful as practiced in the Church; and hence (3) the doctrine of the unifying nature of the liturgical celebrations despite their hierarchical character. The latter, in fact, are not to be considered as private functions, not even with respect to priests and bishops, but as functions of the Church as the "sacrament of unity", namely, as holy People gathered around the bishop and pastor in the communion that makes them *Catholics* and partakers of the unity of the Father, the Son and the Holy Spirit.

Only in this way can we intuitively understand that these acts "pertain to the whole body of the Church; they manifest it and have effects upon it; but they concern the individual members of the Church in different ways, according to their differing rank, office and actual participation" (Art. 26).

On this basis, not only the *plebs Dei* finds its proper place in the Church and in liturgical functions, but even the role of the bishop is better understood while the theology of the Church, prevalent after Vatican Council I, receives completion and equilibrium.

In the Constitution, therefore, there is an intentional, inseparable relationship between article 26, in which the Church is called *sacramentum unitatis* and *plebs sancta sub episcopis adunata et ordinata,* and article 41, in which it is stated that the preeminent manifestation of the Church consists in the full liturgical functions—especially the eucharist—centered around the bishop.

In fact, *if* the Church is that "sacrament of unity" in which men (children of God by right, at present separated from him and from each other because of sin) are again united and ordered around the bishop to be restored as holy People through their sharing in the trinitarian life, *then* it is natural that, speaking concretely and locally, the preeminent realization and expression of the Church is to be found in the very act in which a group of faithful, under their bishop, receives both externally and internally and in the most perfect manner that unity of divine life and realizes that reunion whereby the dispersion caused by sin is overcome.

## II

### THE BISHOP IN AN ECCLESIOLOGY OF SUPERNATURAL
### AND SACRAMENTAL ONTOLOGY

The reunion and unity which make up the Church are a reality preeminently supersensible and supernatural. It is participation in the life, and, therefore, in the unity of the Father, the Son and the Holy Spirit through Christ our Lord.

I say preeminently, but not exclusively. Such a reality, as a matter of fact, by the express will of God, is realized on earth only by means of incarnation: through the medium of human beings and even sensible things. Moreover, it must concern not only the soul but the whole concrete man as an individual and social reality and, hence, in its own way, even the body; indeed, the entire cosmos. It is the law of incarnation freely and wisely willed by God in relation to the world inasmuch as man is a substantial union of spirit and body, even though the latter is subservient to, and the agent of, the former.

Therefore, the reunion and unity that constitute the Church are truly and preeminently a spiritual thing, but also and essentially a human and sensible one, inasmuch as it is incarnate. This is somewhat similar to what happens in man, whose body is an essential part of his nature, inasmuch as it is an inherent part of his whole, even though it is directed and subordinated to the soul.

The sensible aspect of reunion and unity that constitute the Church is represented, among others, by the Scriptures, the hierarchy, the sacraments and all the liturgical celebrations in their sensible aspect.

They are all instruments and an expression of the reunion and inner unity that, in some way, they express and bring about. They are directed and subordinated to it and, along with it, they constitute in its concrete totality, that "carnal and spiritual unity", as St. Ignatius of Antioch[7] calls it, which is the Church.

---

[7] St. Ignatius of Antioch, *Ad Magnes.*12,2: Be subject to the bishop and one to another as Christ is to the Father, according to the flesh, and as the apostles are to Christ and to the Father and to the Holy Spirit, *so that the union may be in flesh and spirit.*

And the Church is *sacramentum unitatis,* according to the patristic and broad meaning of *sacramentum,* inasmuch as its human and sensible aspect is in some way instrumental in manifesting and communicating to men of goodwill that supersensible reality —unity with divine life.

For this very reason the outstanding means of this unity, those that preeminently form the Church and to which the others are directed and subordinated, are strictly speaking the sacraments and, first among them, the eucharist. Indeed, first of all in the sacraments and especially in the eucharist, we find the meaning, content and realization of that reunion of men (in their communion of divine life), which, restoring them to unity, recalls them from the dispersion and disorder of sin into the ordered structure of the Church, and unites them to God and to one another (John 6, 56-7; 1 Cor. 10, 16-7).

The sacraments, nevertheless, cannot be considered apart from the other means established by God. In particular, in order to be effective for the particular individual, they presuppose faith. Their celebration nourishes and expresses faith, hope and charity. Hence, that which saves, confers divine life, brings men together, restores unity and constitutes the Church is neither the sacraments nor faith alone, but faith and the sacraments of faith, first among which is the eucharist. Or, we might say, it is the sacraments, provided that they are taken in their effective concreteness as sacraments of the faith they imply, nourish and manifest.

When we say that the Church realizes and manifests herself mainly in the celebration of the sacraments, above all in the eucharist, we do not mean any celebration but only the one that takes place around the bishop with active participation of the people in full harmony of faith, hope and charity with all that such a celebration presupposes before, during and after the function. Since the sacraments are sacraments of faith, the redeeming celebration of the sacraments that constitutes and manifests the Church is necessarily a celebration of faith.

One thus understands why article 41 states that the main manifestation of the Church is not to be found in any celebration, even the eucharist around the bishop, but in that celebration in which "the full active participation of all God's holy People" is realized. The word "full" here stands for the most perfect possible interior harmony of faith, hope and charity, with all that it presupposes in the pastors and the faithful, as stated above—before, during and after the liturgical function.

We must also note that when the same article treats of the "full active participation of all God's holy People in these liturgical celebrations, especially in the same eucharist, in a single prayer, at one altar, at which there presides the bishop surrounded by his college of priests and by his ministers", it uses a terminology reminiscent of St. Ignatius of Antioch whose ideals are faithfully reflected.[8]

Certainly this ideal is understandable only in the general picture of an ecclesiology in which the ontological aspect of the supernatural and sacramental life is clearly regarded as determinative in its juridical and organizational aspects that are coessential and yet instrumental to it.

It is not an outright rejection, but a necessary modification of a certain theological current in which juridical aspects are too highly emphasized at the expense of other aspects that make up the general picture of the Church.

The Constitution presupposes this ecclesiology of supernatural and sacramental ontology not only in articles 26 and 41 but, to a certain degree, everywhere else.

Article 2, which serves as an ideological preamble to the whole Constitution, develops in a form somewhat different from article 41 the idea that the liturgy, mainly in the eucharistic celebration, is the epiphany par excellence of the Church on earth. The idea is introduced in the perspective of an analysis of the relations between the human visible aspect and the divine invisible aspect of the Church, with special emphasis on the ministerial nature of the human visible aspect over the divine invisible one. It is necessary to reread carefully article 2 in order better to

---

[8] See *Ad Magnes.* 7; *Ad Phil.* 4; *Ad Smyrn.* 8.

understand articles 26 and 41, which treat directly of the bishop. They are passages ideally related, complementing one another.

For the divine liturgy, "through which the work of our redemption is accomplished" most of all in the divine sacrifice of the eucharist, is the outstanding means whereby the faithful may express in their lives, and manifest to others, the mystery of Christ and the real nature of the true Church. It is of the essence of the Church that she be both human and divine, visible and yet invisibly equipped, eager to act and yet intent on contemplation, present in this world and yet not at home in it; and she is all these things in such wise that in her the human is directed and subordinated to the divine, the visible likewise to the invisible, action to contemplation and this present world to that city yet to come, which we seek. While the liturgy daily builds up those who are within into a holy temple of the Lord, into a dwelling place for God in the Spirit, to the mature measure of the fullness of Christ, at the same time it marvelously strengthens their power to preach Christ, and thus shows forth the Church to those who are outside as a sign lifted up among the nations under which the scattered children of God may be gathered together until there is one sheepfold and one shepherd (Art. 2).

Articles 5 to 10 describe the nature of the liturgy and its place in the life of the Church beginning with the reality of Christ who is seen as primal *sacramentum* of salvation—the idea is expressed in biblical and patristic terminology.

The spreading of the good news and the work of redemption of our Lord is continued, we say, first in the preaching and in the sacraments of the "wonderful sacrament of all the Church", thanks to the invisible but efficacious and continuous presence of Christ who, through her, unites us with the Holy Spirit. Thus, we conclude, the exercise of the priesthood of Christ, intended to sanctify men and glorify the Father, is always actual in the liturgy which, even though it does not exhaust the entire activity of the Church, is, nevertheless, the summit to which everything tends as well as the fount whence all her power emanates.

In the Constitution *De Ecclesia* of Vatican Council II, the perspective of supernatural and sacramental ontology aiming at reestablishing a balance with respect to the excessively juridical view is equally clear. It is sufficient to consider the decisive importance given by the Council to baptism in the question of the union of non-Catholic Christians with the true Church, as well as to the eucharist as sacrament that is the Church.

Let us also first consider the recognition given to the episcopate as a true sacrament in which the bishop receives directly from God all the powers needed for the fulfillment of his mission among the faithful, even if the object of this power—that is, the particular subjects over which it is exercised—is assigned directly by the supreme authority of the Church (the pope or the bishops together with the pope) and, secondly, the fact that the exercise of these powers over his particular subjects can, for the common good, be restricted by the same authority.

In the ecclesiology of the Council there is an evident reaction to a too rigid interpretation of the distinction between the power of sanctification and that of jurisdiction, with the tendency to interpret the power of sanctification, centered in the sacrament, in all its true extension of full pastoral power which, after all, includes that of sanctifier as well as that of magisterium in order to safeguard the pontifical primacy.

It is easy to understand how much the liturgical life of the Church is enhanced by this rethinking of the concept of her powers.

### III

#### THE BISHOP AND THE PRINCIPLE THAT THE LITURGY DOES NOT EXHAUST THE ACTIVITY OF THE CHURCH, BUT IS ITS SUMMIT AND FOUNT

What remains is only the consequences of the above-mentioned principles. However, they are indispensable in defining the bishop's role in the liturgy.

In articles 9 and 10 the Constitution states that in substance the liturgy does not exhaust the entire activity of the Church but is the summit toward which this activity is directed and the fount from which all her supernatural power flows. To understand fully the relevance of this statement to the topic we are discussing, it suffices to substitute the word "bishop" for Church.

When the Constitution says that the preeminent realization and manifestation of the Church are in the celebration of the eucharist with full, active participation of all the holy People around their bishop, it is far from trying to set an ideal goal for the pastor in the most intensive performance of rites possible.

Since what saves are not the sacraments alone, but faith coupled with the sacraments, or, we might say, the sacraments of faith, it is more than evident that the bishop must perform many other things besides the liturgical function, true and proper, in order to fulfill his duties of pastor, namely, magisterium, guidance and apostolic actions of all kinds. Otherwise liturgical functions could not produce their full effects in the faithful inasmuch as the latter would perform them without the proper dispositions; they would attend them in a merely exterior fashion and would not draw from them the vigorous consequences they are meant to bring about.

In other words, liturgical celebrations, even if presided over by a bishop, would not take place with that "*full*, active participation of all God's holy People" which, according to article 41 of the Constitution, is the necessary condition for them to be the main realization and manifestation of the Church.

The adjective "full" in article 41 sends us back to articles 11 and 9. Article 11 states: "In order that the liturgy may be able to produce its full effects, it is necessary that the faithful come to it with proper dispositions, that their minds should be attuned to their voices, and that they should cooperate with divine grace lest they receive it in vain."

In article 9 the duties of the pastors with respect to the faithful, even outside the liturgical acts, are forcefully inculcated:

> Before men can come to the liturgy they must be called to faith and to conversion. . . . Therefore the Church announces the good tidings of salvation to those who do not believe. . . . To believers also the Church must ever preach faith and penance; she must prepare them for the sacraments, teach them to observe all that Christ has commanded and invite them to all the works of charity, piety and the apostolate. For all these works make it clear that Christ's faithful, though not of this world, are to be the light of the world and to glorify the Father before men.

But even though not exhausting the entire activity of the Church, "nevertheless the liturgy is the summit toward which the activity of the Church is directed; at the same time it is the fount from which all her power flows" (Art. 10).

The idea is taken up again and rephrased with more precision at the end of the same article: "From the liturgy, therefore, and especially from the eucharist, as from a fount, grace is poured forth upon us; and the sanctification of men in Christ and the glorification of God, to which all other activities of the Church are directed as toward their end, is achieved in the most efficacious possible way."

Let us remember here that the Church is the *plebs sancta sub episcopis adunata et ordinata* (Art. 26). Then we shall understand not only the motives behind the Constitution's assertion that the preeminent manifestation of the Church consists in the full celebration of the eucharist presided over by the bishop, but we shall see also what ideal it sets for each pastor with respect to the liturgy.

How could the Constitution assert of the liturgy, as we have seen above, that it is summit and fount? In the first place because the celebration of the eucharist is the quintessence of the liturgy to which all other sacraments and sacramentals are ordered as to their end. "All the other sacraments seem to be ordered to the eucharist as to their end," says St. Thomas.[9] This is true *a fortiori* of the sacramentals and of the divine office as it is true, and for a still stronger reason, of all the other extra-liturgical activities that take place within the Church.

Now, the eucharist "is the source of all graces", says the catechism of the Council of Trent.[10] ". . . Nor does anyone possess grace before receiving this sacrament except from some desire thereof," adds St. Thomas.[11] Besides, the eucharist as sacrifice of Christ and of the Church is objectively the highest act of glorification that creatures on earth, in the actual order of salvation, can offer to the Creator.

Thus the liturgy—in its very soul, the eucharist—is the highest objective source of grace and glorification of God among the means now at the disposal of man.

After the eucharist the same can be said of the other sacraments because, in virtue of the *opus operatum* the same twofold end of every activity of the Church (the glorification of God and the sanctification of man) is attained through them with the maximum objective effectiveness.

Even the other parts of the liturgy, after the eucharist and the sacraments, attain the mentioned end with objective effectiveness (here we are not concerned with the merit of the subject, which is something completely different) that is superior to the other acts of government, magisterium and apostolate of all kinds that take place in the Church, because they attain it *ex opere operantis Ecclesiae*.[12]

[9] *Summa Theologiae* III q.65 a.3 c
[10] Ed. Roma 1920, n.228.
[11] *Summa Theologiae* III q.79 a.1 ad 1.
[12] See St. Thomas, *Summa Theologiae* III q.82 a.6; a.7 ad 3; IIa-IIae q.83 ad 12.

## IV

### THE BISHOP, HIGH PRIEST OF HIS FLOCK

"The bishop is to be considered as the high priest of his flock, from whom the life in Christ of his faithful is in some way derived and dependent" (Art. 41). The precise meaning of this statement should by now be clear to one who considers it in its immediate context and in that of the Constitution hitherto explained.

This meaning is clear. Because of the bishop's very nature and by the very nature of his specific functions, he must be considered *above all* the high priest of his flock.

This "above all" must be understood in the precise meaning in which we have said that the liturgy does not exhaust all of the Church's activity, but is, nevertheless, the summit and, at the same time, the fount from which springs all its power. This occurs because from the liturgy and particularly from the eucharist, as from a fount, grace pours on us and we obtain with maximum objective effectiveness that sanctification of men and glorification of God toward which all other activities of the Church are directed as to their end.

It has been sufficiently explained that this does not warrant in any way neglecting those ministerial activities that are beyond the liturgical acts, but rather presupposes and demands them. The same is true of the statement that the bishop is above all the high priest of his flock.

That this is truly the meaning of the Constitution is evident from the immediate context of article 41. As a matter of fact, after having said that "the bishop is to be considered as the high priest of his flock, from whom the life in Christ of his faithful is in some way derived and dependent", we say that the liturgical celebrations—particularly the eucharist in which all the people fully participate around the bishop—are "the main manifestation of the Church". If such is the main manifestation of the Church, the bishop (who according to article 26 is the nucleus of reunion and order of this Church) is *above all* the high priest of his flock. Conversely, if the liturgy, without exhausting all the activity of the Church, is nevertheless her summit and fount, the bishop is above all the high priest of his flock.

As the Church is in no other activity more herself than when she is celebrating the eucharist around the bishop in which all of the people participate with full harmony, so the bishop is in no other activity more himself, nor does he fulfill the duties that make him what he is more than during the same celebration. In the performance of that function, above all, he is the shepherd and leader of the scattered children of God whom he thus transforms, or at least he increasingly transforms, into a holy People. He leads them into communion with divine life which, extended to men by the Father through the Son incarnate and in the presence of the Holy Spirit, raises them to the seat of trinitarian life.

If the bishop is above all the high priest of his flock who realizes and manifests himself first of all in presiding over the liturgy and principally in the eucharist, the diocese must be considered above all a structure of ritual and markedly eucharistic value around the bishop.

This seems to be an uncommon idea these days in many regions of the world. But its practical consequences, aiming at the infusion of new vitality into the liturgical life of the diocese (or the cathedral or around the bishop) are numerous. Examples may be found in the feast of the *natalis episcopi,* in that of the dedication of a cathedral, in diocesan ordinations, in the Mass of Holy Chrism, in the just ordering and esteem of the members of one's own diocese.

Therefore, it is undeniable that, along with a jealous preservation of the conscience of the universal Church and of the center of her unity in the Roman pontiff, a reawakening of the sense of the living and concrete reality of the local Church as the means by which every faithful soul inserts himself in the former, can have its own beneficial effects.

For this reason the Constitution, also in article 41, after stating that the bishop is the high priest of his flock, continues: "therefore all should hold in great esteem the liturgical life of the diocese centered around the bishop, especially in his cathedral church."

What has been said of the bishop and of the diocese must be repeated, with due regard for proportions, for the pastor, who is aid and vicar of the bishop in a more limited portion of territory, and for the parish. Even here, the element that informs rather than absorbs and levels all the others must be the liturgy and, markedly, the common celebration of the Sunday mass.

Thus one understands why the Constitution has the article on the diocesan liturgical life follow that on the liturgical life of the parish in an overall perspective similar to the former.

> But because it is impossible for the bishop always and everywhere to preside over the whole flock in his Church, he cannot do other than establish lesser groupings of the faithful. Among these the parishes, set up locally under a pastor who takes the place of the bishop, are the most important; for in some manner they represent the visible Church constituted throughout the world.

> And therefore the liturgical life of the parish and its relationship to the bishop must be fostered theoretically and practically among the faithful and clergy; efforts also must be made to encourage a sense of community within the parish, above all in the common celebration of the Sunday mass (Art. 42).

## CONCLUSION

Three articles of the Instruction on the implementation of the Constitution on the Sacred Liturgy grasp perfectly its deep meaning:

> In the first place, all must be persuaded that the purpose of the Constitution on the Sacred Liturgy of Vatican Council II is not only that of changing the forms and the texts of the liturgy but much more that of bringing about such a formation of faithful and pastoral activity that can find in the liturgy its summit and fount. The changes which have been introduced and those that will, have this purpose.

Therefore, since the liturgy does not exhaust the entire activity of the Church (Art. 9), one must carefully see that the pastoral work be duly connected with it and, at the same time, that the liturgical pastoral activity be not performed in a separate and abstract fashion with respect to the other pastoral activities, but actually be intimately connected with them.

It is especially necessary that an intimate union exist among the liturgy, catechesis, religious instruction and preaching. The bishops, therefore, and their priestly aids should ever more value their entire pastoral mission ordered around the liturgy. Thus the faithful, participating in a perfect way in the holy celebrations, will draw the divine life from them in abundance and, having become leaven of Christ and salt of the earth, they will, in turn, announce and transfuse it into the others.

A spirituality and an overall pastoral activity that should not be reduced to the mere liturgical fact but ordered and centered around the liturgy: this is the ultimate end of the Constitution. The liturgical reformation is a means ordered to this purpose. This rests on the most solid bases of biblical and patristic ecclesiology.

It is easily understood how this, primarily, is going to affect the spirituality and the pastoral activity of the bishops. They are the first to be invested by this new light. They wanted a completion of the ecclesiology of Vatican Council I; now they must accept even the duties it entails.

St. Paul thus sums up his mission and ministry: "I should be a minister of Christ Jesus to the Gentiles; sanctifying the Gospel of God, that the offering up of the Gentiles may become acceptable, being sanctified by the Holy Spirit" (Rom. 15,16).

Two things are greatly detrimental to the liturgy and the apostolate in general as well as to the bishop and the priest: the concept that missionary activity, the spreading of the Gospel in its broader meaning, is independent of liturgical reality in its strict sense, and the view that the liturgy in its strict sense is independent of the apostolic and missionary reality in its broader sense.

St. Paul in the text mentioned speaks directly of the apostolate, which he describes in liturgical and sacrificial terms, inasmuch as he considers it in a liturgical and sacrificial perspective: the purpose of the apostolate is to make an acceptable offering of men to God, sanctified by the Holy Spirit.

It is not arbitrary, on our part, to extend this Pauline view to the liturgical celebrations and eucharistic sacrifice properly so-called. In fact, in the eucharistic celebration presided over by the apostle and with full participation of the people, that offering of men gathered in Christ from the dispersion of sin which is accepted and sanctified by the Holy Spirit and is the end of any apostolate and episcopate, takes place in its most perfect and objective way.

This is what the Constitution of Vatican Council II means when it repeats: "For the aim and object of apostolic works is that all who are made sons of God by faith and baptism should come together to praise God in the midst of his Church, to take part in the sacrifice, and to eat the Lord's supper" (Art. 10).

The union of mission and liturgy, of reunited people and liturgy in order to arrive at a liturgical mission and a missionary liturgy—this is, in sum, the great message of Vatican Council II in this field.

---

## JOSEPH PASCHER

Born September 26, 1893 in Hertlingen, Germany. He was ordained in 1916, and earned his doctorate in philosophy at the University in Frankfurt am Main in 1921 and his doctorate in theology at the Universities of Giessen and Würzburg. His published works are mainly concerned with liturgical subjects and the spiritual life. He is co-editor of the *Münchener Theologischen Studien* and collaborates in several liturgical reviews.

Joseph Pascher/*Munich, W. Germany*

# Relation between Bishop and Priests according to the Liturgy Constitution

The Constitution on the Sacred Liturgy of Vatican Council II gives the bishop a share in the right to regulate the liturgy (Art. 22, 1). But the legislative power of the bishop, of which this regulation of the liturgy is a part, is itself based on a more profound theological relationship between the bishop, his priests and his faithful: "The bishop is to be considered as the high priest of his flock, from whom the life in Christ of his faithful is in some way derived and dependent" (Art. 41). Yet, in ordinary church life the faithful usually look on themselves rather as connected with the "presbyter", the priest. The Council treats the priest in liturgical actions as representative of the bishop and desires a deepening of that "liturgical life of the parish and its relationship to the bishop [which] must be fostered theoretically and practically among the faithful and clergy" (Art. 42).

It is therefore obviously important to give some thought to the relationship between bishop and priest. The problem concerns particularly the relationship between the local bishop and the priest who celebrates the liturgy within his territory, whether this priest lives in the immediate presence of the bishop or not.

Historically speaking, at least, the priest would normally belong to that body of priests that surrounds the local bishop.

As soon as history mentions bishop and priest together, the priest is seen in the framework of a "college", as part of the *synedrium* of the bishop, for instance, in Ignatius of Antioch (d. 107 A.D.; *Ad Magn.* 6,1; *Ad Trall.* 3,1; *Ad Philad.* 8,1). Ignatius calls the bishop the image of the Father and the priest the image of the apostle. Perhaps he was thinking of the text about the elders in Apocalypse 4,4.

The liturgy is the concern of the bishop: "Let no man do aught of things pertaining to the Church apart from the bishop. Let that be held a valid eucharist that is under the bishop or one to whom he shall have committed it. Wheresoever the bishop shall appear, there let the people be" (*To the Smyrnaeans,* n.8, tr. Lightfoot). Perhaps he saw in his mind the community singing the liturgy when he wrote with some enthusiasm: "For your honorable presbytery . . . is attuned to the bishop, even as its strings to a lyre. Therefore in your concord and harmonious love Jesus Christ is sung" (*To the Ephesians,* n.4, tr. Lightfoot).

In the threefold gradation of Ignatius' community the deacon does not belong to the *synedrium*. This provides the apostolic tradition of Hippolytus, about a century later, with a theological argument for the distinction between the place of the deacon and that of the priest: "At the ordination of the deacon only the bishop lays on his hands because the deacon is not ordained to the priesthood but to the service of the bishop whose commands he executes. For the deacon does not belong to the council of the clergy" (ed. Botte, p. 22).

The deacon, too, has the *Pneuma,* but not in the same way as the priest: *non accipiens communem praesbyterii spiritum eum cuius participes praesbyteri sunt.* At the ordination of a priest the other priests share in the laying on of hands with the bishop *propter communem et similem cleri spiritum* (ed. Botte, p. 24). This joint possession of the Spirit creates a close link between bishop and presbyterium. This is shown at the consecration of a bishop. The priests cannot take part in the laying on of hands, but afterward it is they, and not the other bishops, who celebrate the eucharist jointly with their new head: "The deacons bring the offerings to him, and, jointly with all his priests, he stretches his hands out over them and pronounces the eucharistic prayer" (ed. Botte, p. 10).

The concession that the eucharist may also be celebrated by "one committed by the bishops" (*To the Smyrnaeans*, n.8) operates against this unity of bishop and presbyterium in a centrifugal way. When the bishop is prevented, or when the diocese expands and the number of faithful is too large, the priests must be sent out, at least for the celebration of the eucharist on Sundays. In 416 A.D. Innocent I wrote to Decentius that priests belonging to a Roman *titulus* should not think they were separated from the papal celebration when on Sundays they celebrated the eucharist for the faithful in their own churches.

The eucharistic unity would then be maintained by the sending of the *fermentum,* a host consecrated by the pope (c.5). The old law demanded that the priests should be with their bishop, particularly on the Sunday, the proper day for the celebration of the eucharist (*Apost. Const.* II, 57,4). But in the Rome of Innocent I this unity was already so much diluted for the priests attached to the cemeteries near the city that they had to celebrate by themselves. The custom of the *fermentum* persisted in Rome until within the 9th century: "During this night (Easter) the cardinal-priests are not present but each celebrates mass in his own titular church . . . Each one sends a priest sacristan from his titular church to the church of the Redeemer [the basilica of the Lateran]. There they wait till the breaking of the host . . . Then comes the *subdiaconus oblationarius* and gives them a particle of the *sancta,* the host consecrated by the pope. They wrap it in their corporal, and each returns to his titular church and hands the *sancta* to the priest. He makes the sign of the cross over the chalice, puts the *sancta* into it and says: *Dominus vobiscum* (*O.R.* XXX B,64,65).

For the popes who followed this custom of the *fermentum,* the sending of the consecrated bread was a sacramental and true symbol of unity: "Because there is one loaf, we though many are one body, for we all partake of the same loaf" (1 Cor. 10, 17). This rite of dropping a particle of the consecrated host into the chalice is even today particularly significant insofar as it expresses, within the symbolism of the eucharist, the unity of bishop and presbyterium.

This custom of the *fermentum* with its full meaning persisted longest in the ordination to the priesthood. The priest is ordained for a particular church and goes there at once: "The bishop takes whole eucharistic loaves and distributes them among all the newly ordained priests, who communicate from them for eight days" (9th century, *O.R.* XXXVI, 23).

Apart from the *fermentum* the Roman Church also knew the concelebration of priests with their bishop. It is, however, doubtful whether the joint recitation of the canon represents an old tradition, in spite of Amalarius of Metz who thinks that it was a Roman custom *ut in confectione immolationis Christi assint Presbyteri, et simul cum Pontifice verbis et manibus conficiant* (*Lib. off.* I, 12,25).

At best we have a 7th-century text that says: "On feast days, *i.e.*, Easter, Pentecost, St. Peter's and Christmas—on these four feasts the cardinal-priests come together for the celebration. Each has a corporal in his hand, and the archdeacon comes round and gives them each three *oblata*. When the Pontifex proceeds to the altar, they surround the altar, right and left, and recite the canon together with the Pontifex . . . And they consecrate jointly the body and blood of the Lord" (*O.R.* III, 1). In the 13th century Innocent III said that "sometimes many priests celebrate together" and that "the cardinal-priests surround the Roman pontiff and are wont to celebrate likewise with him" (*De s. altaris myst.* IV,20).

The pontifical of the Roman curia (13th century) has the concelebration at the ordination of a priest, but not the *fermentum*. There is an unmistakable hesitation: "They pronounce everything in an undertone as if they were celebrating" (*Pont. curiae* X, 34). A little earlier Thomas Aquinas shows no awareness of an old tradition when he comments on the "use of some churches": *Sicut apostoli Christo coenanti concoenaverunt, ita novi ordinati episcopo ordinanti concelebrant* (*Summa Theologiae* III, q. 82, a.2). A decisive factor was that Durandus of Mende (d. 1296) incorporated concelebration at the consecration of a bishop and at the ordination of a priest in his pontifical, though not compulsory in the latter case: "The ordained may, if they wish, have books in front of them, and in a low tone pronounce the canon and all those parts of the mass said by the ordaining bishop" (XIII, 20).

Where outside Rome, concelebration with the bishop on certain feast days was accepted under the influence of the Roman *Ordines,* the custom lasted longer and without being tied to ordinations, particularly in France. Around 1700 de Moléon was able to observe concelebration in several French cities on great feasts (*Voyages liturgiques de France,* Lyons, p. 231). The manner of concelebration may be gathered from his description of such a solemnity in the church of St. Moritz, Vienna: *Les six prêtres assistants récitoient le canon avec l'évêque et faisoient les mêmes signes que lui, selon qu'il est marqué dans l'Ordinaire de l'église cathédrale de l'an 1524: Suburbani signa faciant durante Missa ad modum Episcopi; et sic in omnibus maioribus festivitatibus* (p. 17). Apart from the complete rite this keen observer also noticed a step backward. In the cathedral of Orleans the words of the consecration were excluded from the joint recitation.

In the history of the Latin Church there is no evidence of a concelebration without a bishop. Vatican Council II, therefore, introduces something new insofar as it introduces a concelebration of priests without even demanding a representative of the bishop as chief celebrant (Art. 57). Since, however, it is for the bishop to regulate the discipline of concelebration in his diocese, he is still always free to appoint the chief celebrant as his representative and so to make clergy and laity more aware of the cohesion of bishop and priests, as implied in article 41.

This growing autonomy of the priest is not only visible in the celebration of the eucharist. Baptism and penance—particularly penance—were originally also an episcopal preserve. Ordinary practical needs made it very soon imperative for the priest to be authorized to baptize. The growth toward complete autonomy proceeded here in different stages. Not until the 11th century did the priest become the normal minister of the first sacrament.

In Rome itself it is again among the priests of the titular churches that the old law remains observable longer than elsewhere. In the 12th century, according to the Ordo of Benedict of St. Peter, they apply to the pope on Holy Saturday for permission to administer baptism (c. 43). In baptism the bishop's right was based on the fact that it concerns a sacrament of initiation.

This counts also for the sacrament of penance that, according to the early Christian view, meant re-admission into the Church from which the penitent had previously been expelled. Here the development of administration by the priest grew much more slowly because in the first centuries the sacrament of penance was very rarely administered. The old law has left traces even today in the liturgy of the ordination of a priest insofar as the imposition of hands, which imparts the power of absolution, is a separate action introduced much later and not integrated in the ordination proper, like the power to celebrate. Even this action of the bishop does not yet really give the newly ordained priest the power to absolve. This is given to the priest by a special commission, independent of the ordination.

How in the case of confirmation, too, pastoral needs led to commissioning the ordinary priests, is well known. The strength of the bishop's rights in this matter has had a decisive influence on the institution of assistant bishops (Weihbischöfe). Unless all the facts are misleading, the Church today has to face the problem of whether it would not be better here also to steer toward administration by priests, and this in the interest of the episcopal function itself for which the assistant bishop (Weihbischöf) without a presbyterium and without a community constitutes a difficulty. It is significant that the meaningful words used by the

Constitution to describe the bishop's place and function all apply to the resident local bishop (esp. Art. 41 and 42).

The group of cardinal-priests is all that remains in Rome of the ancient college of priests. Yet, the image that the old Church had of its structure is blurred by the fact that these cardinal-priests are at the same time bishops. In the dioceses of the old world there is at least a kind of presbyterium in the cathedral chapters. Canon law echoes Ignatius when it refers to these canons as the *senatus et consilium* of the bishop (Can. 391,1). In the projected reform of the code of canon law one might well investigate whether the relationship between chapter and bishop corresponds to an ideal constitution of the Church.

As a theological fact, all priests of the diocese belong to the bishop's presbyterium and work entirely under his mandate if they wish their work to be "valid" in the Ignatian sense. The bishop can only fulfill the extraordinary mission laid upon him in article 41 of the Liturgical Constitution through his presbyterium, and if the presbyterium puts itself unconditionally at his disposal. The bishops of today more and more seek a close understanding with their priests. This is ultimately a matter of restoring the presbyterium of old. The reference in the Constitution to liturgical fulfillment that asks for a deeper awareness in thought and action of the relationship between liturgical life and the function of the bishop (Art. 42), applies to all life in the Church. The new canon law should take that into account. However, as laws are not enough, the heart must be stirred to see the ideal image of the Church in the pattern of the Mystical Body: one bishop, one priesthood, one community.

# FREDERICK R. McMANUS

Born February 8, 1923, he was educated at Holy Cross College, Worcester, Mass. and at St. John's Seminary, Brighton, Mass., and was ordained in 1947 for the diocese of Boston, Mass. He pursued his studies at the Catholic University of America, Wash., D.C., and earned his doctorate in 1954 with the thesis, "The Congregation of Sacred Rites". He is editor of *The Jurist,* associate editor of the *Yearbook of Liturgical Studies,* and since 1958 has been professor of canon law at the Catholic University of America. His published works include *The Rites of Holy Week,* 1956; *Handbook for the New Rubrics,* 1961; *Revival of the Liturgy,* 1963.

Frederick R. McManus/*Washington, D.C., U.S.A.*

# The Juridical Power of the Bishop in the Constitution on the Sacred Liturgy

The key statement in the Constitution on the Liturgy affecting the juridical power of the bishop is article 22. Attributing the regulation of the sacred liturgy to the Apostolic See and, *ad normam iuris,* to the bishop (Art. 22, 1), the article stands in sharp contrast to canon 1257 (C.I.C.), which before Vatican Council II summed up the development of liturgical authority in the Latin Church: "It pertains to the Apostolic See alone to order the sacred liturgy and to approve the liturgical books." Probably more significant for the future evolution of episcopal power in the Church, the same article acknowledges the right to regulate the liturgy "within certain defined limits" as residing in "various kinds of competent territorial bodies of bishops legitimately established" (Art. 22, 2).

Nevertheless, the starting point for any first attempt to appraise the juridical power possessed by bishops after the enactment of the Constitution must be doctrinal. Canon law, both as a body of norms and as a science, has too long suffered from its divorce from theology, too long appeared as something foreign to the inner mystery of the Church.[1] The causes for this situation, whether the influences of secular legal systems or the weaknesses of theological speculation, are not at issue here. Any general appraisal of the new Constitution from a canonical viewpoint would reveal a compromise and development: the retention of sacrosanct terminology and institutes, combined with a fresh breadth and flexibility. The latter flow from a genuine return to evangelical and patristic sources; they are suited to norms guiding the Christian life of the free children of God.

In the case of the juridical figure of the bishop, the doctrinal background supplied by the Constitution is particularly rich. The Church of God is defined as "the holy People united and ordered under their bishops" (Art. 26), in the language of St. Cyprian.[2] The bishop "is to be considered as the high priest of his flock, from whom the life in Christ of his faithful is in some way derived and dependent" (Art. 41).

This relationship of the holy People to the bishop (and with his cooperators who together with the bishop are the *servi* in the eucharistic prayer) is seen in his presidential office, upon which the Constitution lays new and welcome stress. The Council sees in the liturgical assembly the "preeminent manifestation of the Church . . . the full active participation of all God's holy People in these liturgical celebrations, especially in the same eucharist, in a single prayer, at one altar, at which there presides the bishop surrounded by his college of priests and by his ministers" (Art. 41).

A consequence of this in the concrete is the restoration of concelebration (Art. 57). If a priest presides in the role of chief celebrant, he does so always in the bishop's place: "Because it is impossible for the bishop always and everywhere to preside over the whole flock in his Church, he cannot do other than establish lesser groupings of the faithful. Among these the parishes, set up locally under a pastor who takes the place of the bishop, are the

[1] Cf. H. V. Cann, "Changing Emphases in the Concept of Authority in the Church," in *The Jurist* 23 (1963), pp. 391-3.

[2] St. Cyprian, *On the Unity of the Catholic Church*, 7; cf. Letter 66, n. 8,3 as cited in the notes to the Constitution.

most important. . . . The liturgical life of the parish and its relationship to the bishop must be fostered theoretically and practically among the faithful and clergy. . . ." [3]

This extensive and nonjuridical introduction to the topic seems
essential because the sacred canons, especially in their modern
codification, treat episcopal power (and most canonical institutes) in a legal vacuum. The life and customs of the People of
God in its earthly pilgrimage are rightly clothed and indeed directed by juridical formulations, which have great benefits: clarity, precision, system, a balance of unity and diversity, an evol-
ving Christian *aequitas*. But a strong beginning must always be
made, treating the law in the light of the Church as mystery, as
sign of God's hidden plan now revealed in Christ, if only to coun-
teract the threat of legalism, rigidity, formalism, legislation for
the sake of law-making, and the like.

### REGULATORY POWER OF THE BISHOP

It is too early to attempt any exhaustive commentary upon
article 22 of the Constitution and its ramifications, much less to
predict future developments. Its text, however, should be carefully scrutinized in the whole setting of the conciliar document
and of the Council itself.

The first paragraph of article 22 states: "Regulation of the
sacred liturgy depends solely on the authority of the Church, that
is, on the Apostolic See and, *ad normam iuris,* on the bishop." [4]
Although these words appear in a section of Chapter I devoted to
the "general norms" of liturgical reform (Art. 22-25), they are
broader in their application: the entire moderation, regulation
and ordination of the liturgy depend on the authority of the
Church; this authority resides in the Apostolic See and in the

---

[3] Art. 42. Cf. J. D. Crichton, *The Church's Worship: Considerations on
the Liturgical Constitution of the Second Vatican Council* (New York:
Sheed & Ward, 1964), pp. 75-9.

[4] *Sacrae Liturgiae moderatio ab Ecclesiae auctoritate unice pendet:
quae quidem est apud Apostolicam Sedem et, ad normam iuris, apud
Episcopum.*

bishop—that is, in the chief bishop, the pope and in the individual bishop.

Curiously, the wording is precise in one particular, loose in another. "Apostolic See", for all its canonical implications (Can. 7), does not parallel "bishop"—and "Apostolic See" alongside "episcopal see" would have required even more explanation. But the word "bishop", in the singular, is precisely chosen to indicate that each bishop has genuine authority and regulatory power over the sacred liturgy. There was no need to say that the whole body of bishops, the apostolic college assembled in union with the chief bishop, possesses supreme power over the universal Church (Can. 228, 1) in matters of worship; there was need to recognize a measure of power in the individual bishop presiding over his flock.

The contrast to canon 1257, which attributes this power exclusively to the Apostolic See, is obvious. As a matter of fact, pontifical documents subsequent to the code of canon law have, if anything, asserted an even greater reservation of power. Canon 1257 may imply that only the Apostolic See can approve particular or local liturgical books; in 1958 this was asserted explicitly ("books duly approved by the Apostolic See, whether for the universal Church, or for some particular Church or religious family") and even made the basis for a distinction between liturgical services and *pia exercitia* (S.R.C., Instr. Sept. 3, 1955, n. 12). This was the canonical counterpart of Pius XII's teaching in *Mediator Dei* of 1947: ". . . the supreme pontiff alone has the right to permit or establish any liturgical practice, to introduce or approve new rites, or to make any changes in them he considers necessary" (*A.A.S.* 39 [1947] 544).

Prior to the enactment of the Constitution, the juridical power of the bishop in relation to the liturgy was better expressed as a duty rather than as a right: ". . . to enforce vigilantly the observance of the canonical rules on divine worship" (*A.A.S.* 39 [1947] 544). Negatively, the authority was more extensive, to correct abuses and superstitious practices, according to the terms of canon 1261—which does acknowledge episcopal power to exercise legislative authority for the enforcement of the discipline of sacred worship (Can. 1261, 1), and to visit places of cult otherwise exempt from episcopal jurisdiction in certain circumstances (Can. 1261, 2). To this might be added the instances, of greater or less significance, of specific concessions, faculties, and the like possessed by the individual bishop (Can. 755, 2; 759, 2; 1156; 1274, 1; 1275; 1292).

The Constitution goes beyond all this and sets down, as norm and principle, the regulatory power of the bishop affecting the liturgy. The fact that this is a broad statement and that its development for the future is unpredictable does not lessen its significance: without specifying limits or details, Vatican Council II recognizes a juridical power in the bishop which in the past was difficult or impossible to vindicate.

What is the meaning of the expression *ad normam iuris* in this context? First, it should be noted that the Council does not enter into the question of the origin of the regulatory power, whether the law mentioned is human or divine. At the same time, article 22 may be viewed as a step in the direction of the argument offered by some Fathers of the Council, among them Cardinal Ritter of St. Louis,[5] that each bishop should be acknowledged to have all the authority needed to fulfill his mission, except that which the pope for good reasons reserves to himself. Thus the presumption would no longer be that the bishop lacks power until it is conceded to him in some particular, but that he has power unless or until the supreme pontiff reserves the matter to himself.

Whatever the development in the broad field of pontifical-episcopal relationships, the almost absolute papal reservation of power over public worship has been relaxed by the Constitution on the Liturgy. And it is also worthy of note that Pope Paul VI drew attention to this particular article in the apostolic letter of January 25, 1964, on the execution of the Constitution (Motu Proprio *Sacram Liturgiam,* n. XI).

[5] Nov. 7, 1963. Cf. J. W. Baker, "Implications of Collegiality," in *The Jurist* 24 (1964), p. 255.

The second point to be made about the phrase, *ad normam iuris,* is the way in which the law of the Constitution does specify some of the episcopal powers in relation to the liturgy. An enumeration of these is thus in order next.

## SPECIFIC EPISCOPAL POWERS IN RELATION TO THE LITURGY

In many places the Constitution places heavy obligations upon the individual bishop, for example, to reform seminary teaching (Art. 15-17; *Motu Proprio,* n. I), to help priests already in the ministry to understand, live and share the liturgical life (Art. 18), to promote liturgical instruction for, and participation by, the faithful (Art. 19). Here, however, the instances of power attributed to the bishop by the Council should be listed.

An important article of Chapter I speaks of the special dignity of the devotions "proper to particular Churches" provided these are celebrated "by mandate of the bishops according to customs or books lawfully approved" (Art. 13). At first glance it may seem that this authority over sacred celebrations in their own churches or dioceses is little more than what is acknowledged in the code (Can. 1259, 1); in fact, without prejudging the matter, the Council is strengthening the status of those services of public worship celebrated under the bishop's authority and presidency, even though not part of the official service books of the Roman liturgy. These are more and more carefully to be distinguished from private devotions, and to be drawn closer to the liturgical spirit (Cf. Art. 13).

Specific instances, too, of episcopal authority are mentioned in the same chapter: in the matter of radio and television transmission of sacred rites "under the leadership and direction of a suitable person appointed for this office by the bishops" (Art. 20); over the Bible services, the "sacred celebrations of the word of God", with the rule: "where no priest is available . . . a deacon or some other person authorized by the bishop should preside . . ." (Art. 35, 4); in the direction of the diocesan liturgi-

cal commission (Art. 45) and the other commissions on music
and art (Art. 46).

It is in Chapter II, however, on the mystery of the eucharist,
that the Council begins to work out the balance of power with
regard to individual liturgical rites. Adhering to the doctrine of
Trent but not its discipline, the Constitution states: " . . . communion under both kinds may be granted when the bishops think
fit, not only to clerics and religious, but also to the laity, in cases
to be determined by the Apostolic See . . ." (Art. 55). Two
points need to be made:

(1) Perhaps we have here an example of the easing of ten-
sion between universal norms and local needs and ways. The
Apostolic See, through the newly created *Consilium* for the implementation of the Constitution (*Motu Proprio*), will determine
broadly the cases, of which the Constitution lists only instances,
for communion under both kinds; thus the outer limits of this
reform, in its experimental stage, will be set for the entire Latin
Church. In turn, the individual bishop will have authority over
the reformed discipline; he will be able to accept or reject the
specific cases—always, it may be hoped, for pastoral reasons
and with the aim of making the sign of the eucharist ever more
meaningful and effective.

(2) Unlike the next case, that of concelebration, the power
resides exclusively in the bishops, without mention of other ordinaries. The reform is momentous; religious, for example, do
not have a greater stake in it than the rest of the faithful; and
the judgment is left to the bishop.

Chapter II also goes into some detail with regard to the restoration of concelebration in full ritual or sacramental form. This
time the judgment is left to the bishops and to other ordinaries,
both local and religious, in cases where permission is needed
(Art. 57, 1, 2). The liberality of the Council in its measures of
liturgical reform was matched by a desire not to impose unknown
and unwelcome usages in areas where, for example, clerical training and background are weak. Thus concelebration was restored
as the universal practice for the Holy Thursday masses, for

councils, synods, and episcopal conferences, and for the blessing of an abbot (Art. 57, 1), but all other cases were left dependent upon permission.

Article 57 of the Constitution encountered a certain measure of opposition, particularly in the section referring to the needed "permission of the ordinary". The vote was 1839 affirmative, 315 negative (Oct. 10, 1963). Part of the opposition was due, as later transpired, to a strong preference of an even larger number of bishops for "permission of the local ordinary".

This may have resulted from general feeling, in a much broader context, that the privilege of exemption from episcopal jurisdiction should be diminished. Or the bishops may not have been satisfied with the provisions of the present code which in fact allow them to intervene to correct abuses or violations of diocesan legislation concerning divine cult (Can. 1261, 2). In any event, the Conciliar Commission clarified the matter by rewording the article so that both bishops and religious ordinaries may permit concelebration, but the ultimate moderation of its discipline belongs to the bishop alone: "The regulation, however, of the discipline of concelebration in the diocese pertains to the bishop" (Art. 57, 2, 1). Such an affirmation admirably links the role of the bishop in the eucharist, presiding over the (con-) celebration or deputing another to preside in his place, with his juridical power over the liturgical discipline (Cf. Art. 41-42).

In the chapter on the other sacraments and the sacramentals, three articles refer to episcopal authority:

(1) The restored liturgical catechumenate is to be employed "at the discretion of the local ordinary" (Art. 64).

(2) Variants in the baptismal rite when there are large numbers of candidates are to be used, again, "at the discretion of the local ordinary" (Art. 68).

(3) Reservation of blessings "shall be in favor only of bishops or ordinaries"; and certain specified sacramentals will be available for celebration by lay persons only "at the discretion of the ordinary" (Art. 79).

The first and third of these deserve some comment. Article 64, speaking of the restored liturgical catechumenate, leaves local determination in the hands of the bishop or other local ordinary. This confirms the norm for the use of the 1963 rite of this kind,[6] but looks forward to a sound integration of the period of instruction and formation of converts with the liturgical rites in which the whole community has a part.

The terms of article 79, concerned with sacramentals, encountered the same hesitations on the part of the conciliar Fathers as had the right of religious ordinaries to permit concelebration, according to article 57, 1b. To begin with, it was necessary for the Conciliar Commission to make it clear that the only reservations to religious contemplated in article 79 were of rites to be celebrated by the religious ordinaries themselves for the benefit of the exempt religious alone, for example, the blessing of a sacred place pertaining to a clerical exempt religious institute. The pastoral intent of the second paragraph of article 79 is to suppress all privileged reservations that obstruct priests in the parochial ministry from serving the faithful fully; this is not hurt by the appropriate reservation to bishops of more solemn blessings.

The highly limited and almost tentative plan to assign some sacramentals for administration by qualified lay persons is left for its implementation to the "ordinary" rather than to bishops or local ordinaries alone (Art. 79). In fact, however, it is local ordinaries who would exercise such judgment generally, since the lay persons in question would be subject to their authority; the wording of the Constitution would make an exception for lay religious who might receive such a permission from their religious ordinaries.

The two instances of episcopal power mentioned in Chapter IV on the divine office are shared with other local ordinaries and with religious ordinaries. This is understandable since both (1) dispensations and commutations in regard to the office (Art.

[6] April 16, 1963, *Ordo Baptismi Adultorum per Gradus Catechumenatus Dispositus*, Normae, n. 1.

97; *Motu Proprio,* n. VII), and (2) permission to use the mother tongue in the office celebrated by clerics (Art. 101, 1; *Motu Proprio* n. IX) are matters of equal concern to religious ordinaries and bishops. The first of these norms corrects the paradoxical situation that bishops, although the chief moderators of divine cult in their dioceses, could find no authority in the written law to justify their granting dispensations and commutations that were readily conceded by religious superiors and others.

There is certainly nothing in these articles of the Constitution on the Liturgy to suggest any wholesale transfer of powers formerly exercised by the Apostolic See to the individual bishops. Even if, gradually or through the specific determination of a conciliar decree in a forthcoming session of the Council, a presumption of authority in the individual bishop is acknowledged unless or until a matter is specifically reserved by the pope, the great issue of liturgical reformation is hardly one to be determined in each local church.

Nevertheless, Vatican Council II gives substantial recognition to the liturgical authority of the individual bishop, especially in article 22, 1. This juridical power flows from the liturgical office of the bishop. Its enunciation in terms of law is not unrelated to the position taken by the vast majority of the conciliar Fathers on the basis of the sacred office: 2123 voted, with 34 opposed, that the schema *De Ecclesia* should be drawn up so as to state that episcopal consecration constitutes the highest grade of the sacrament of holy orders; 2049 voted, with 104 opposed, that the same schema should be drawn up so as to state that every bishop legitimately consecrated into the community of the bishops and of the Roman pontiff, who is its head and principle of unity is a member of the body of bishops.[7]

[7] Oct. 30, 1963. Cf. *Herder Correspondence,* Jan. 1964, p. 12. Since this article is directly concerned with the juridical power of the bishop in the Constitution on the Liturgy, that is, in terms of the Council's progress through its second period (1963), the subsequent developments in the third period (1964) concerning this power are not treated. They involve: (1) the Constitution on the Church, and (2) the Decree on the Pastoral Office of Bishops in the Church (formerly called "Bishops and the Government of Dioceses").

## REGIONAL EXERCISE OF JURIDICAL POWER

The mention above of the general liturgical reform brings us to the second paragraph of the same article 22 of the Constitution. However great the trend toward decentralization of the exercise of sacred authority in the Church, it is completely unrealistic to suppose a diversity of rites and usages on a purely local or diocesan level. When in fact examples are sought of areas of ecclesiastical jurisdiction which might well be exercised on a regional or national basis, the moderation or regulation of public worship is always among the first examples offered.

If it is desirable, for instance, that the reformed liturgical books provide facultative rubrics, with the choice at the discretion of the individual bishop (or, for that matter, in lesser matters left to the judgment of the individual celebrant), it is clear that substantive adaptations must be on a regional basis (Cf. Art. 39-40). Only in this way can a reasonable uniformity throughout moderately large areas be obtained, and this degree of uniformity is called for by the development of modern communications, mobility of populations, etc.

The starting point for this kind of decentralization—and the restoration to the Church, in a new dress and with fresh vigor, of the venerable discipline of councils and synods—is the second paragraph of article 22: "In virtue of power conceded by the law, the regulation of the liturgy within certain defined limits belongs also to various kinds of competent territorial bodies of bishops legitimately established." [8]

Some have argued that the regional exercise of juridical power by bodies of bishops, whether in the provincial and plenary councils of the past or in the bodies, generally called conferences, of this century, is not a manifestation of "collegiality", since the whole apostolic college is not involved. The Fathers of Vatican Council II appear to feel otherwise. Their attitude on the doctrine of collegiality is evident enough: 1108 voted, with 336 opposed,

[8] *Ex potestate a iure concessa, rei liturgicae moderatio inter limites statutos pertinet quoque ad competentes varii generis territoriales Episcoporum coetus legitime constitutos.*

that the schema *De Ecclesia* should be drawn up so as to state
that the college of bishops has the ministry of evangelizing, sanctifying and caring for the flock, is the successor of the college of
apostles, and, together with its head, the Roman pontiff, and
never without this head (whose right of primacy over all pastors
and faithful remains untouched and undiminished) is endowed
with full and supreme power over the universal Church; 1717
voted, with 408 opposed, that the same schema should be drawn
up so as to state that this authority that pertains to the college
of bishops in union with its head is by divine right.[9] The same
conciliar Fathers then moved from doctrine to discipline, and
found in the juridical constitution of episcopal conferences (in
the schema *De Episcopis et Dioecesium Regimine*) the concrete
manifestation, region by region or nation by nation, of this same
corporate responsibility of all the bishops over all the churches.

If each bishop has a solicitude for the churches other than
his own, this concern is the stronger in relation to the dioceses
of the province, of the region, of the nation. How such a solicitude or care will be expressed juridically, if at all, is something
else again, but it is a manifestation of the collegial character of
the community of bishops, even on the regional level.

The past manifestation of this almost natural phenomenon in
the Church has taken the form of patriarchates and provinces,
synods and councils (Can. 281, 283). Now the less formally
structured conferences, almost unknown in the codification of
canon law,[10] receive the recognition of the Ecumenical Council.

In article 22, 2, the Council carefully refrains from entering
into any doctrinal question as to the place of such conferences or
bodies of bishops in the constitution of the Church; the origin of
the "power conceded by law", whether human or divine, is simply
not specified. Similarly, the Council refrains from prejudging the
various species of existing episcopal conferences, leaving this
properly to the subsequent constitution *De Episcopis et Dioece-*

---

[9] Oct. 30, 1963. Cf. *Herder Correspondence, loc. cit.*
[10] Can. 292; cf. Can. 1507, 1; 1909, 1; *Ordo Baptismi Adultorum . . . ,*
Normae, n. 3, 5-6; *Codex Rubricarum*, n. 117.

*sium Regimine.* This is the sense of the attribution of power to "various kinds of competent territorial bodies of bishops legimately constituted". Lest the Constitution on the Liturgy remain ineffective for a period of time in some of its principal facets, until the Council is able to determine the nature and juridical status of episcopal conferences, the right to regulate the liturgy was acknowledged as present in various kinds of such bodies.

When article 22 was under consideration by the Council, it was pointed out that the power spoken of in the text might be exercised by provincial conferences of bishops, provincial and plenary councils, existing national or regional groupings of bishops, etc., provided only that these were lawfully constituted. On January 25, 1964, Pope Paul VI issued an interim disposition for the bodies of bishops, to be followed in their exercise of legislative authority over the liturgy (*Motu Proprio,* n. X):

(1) In the interim, *i.e.,* until the completion of the expected Constitution on the subject, the authority of article 22, 2, is possessed by *national* bodies of bishops. This does not preclude the association of the bishops of several nations in a single group for concerted action; it does withhold, at least for the present, the operation of such bodies on a basis smaller than national, although this may be of great importance in bilingual and multilingual regions and countries.

(2) In addition to residential bishops, those mentioned (or referred to) in canon 292 (C.I.C.) have the right by law to participate and to vote. Coadjutor and auxiliary bishops may be called to the conferences.

(3) For the exercise of the legislative power, a two-thirds majority, by secret ballot, is required.

The second and third provisions have importance as derived substantially from the schema *De Episcopis et Dioecesium Regimine.* The entire disposition of the Pope enables the full exercise of the power of article 22, 2 without delay.

### "Certain Defined Limits" of Juridical Power

What are the "certain defined limits" of the juridical power of the national episcopates? Prescinding from preconciliar faculties affecting the liturgy (with regard to the color of vestments [Codex Rubricarum, n. 117] and to adaptations and the use of the vernacular in the rite for the adult catechumenate[11]) we may enumerate the following from the Constitution itself:

(1) The power to determine the extent of the mother tongue to be used in the liturgy (Art. 36, 3), as well as to approve the vernacular translation for liturgical rites (Art. 36, 4). For the former, the acts of the conference must be confirmed (*actis probatis seu confirmatis*) by the Apostolic See; for the latter, the Constitution requires no confirmation, although one interpretation of the January *Motu Proprio* asserts such confirmation is needed.[12] Other articles of the Constitution specify the limits of episcopal authority, within the structure of the territorial bodies or conferences, for the concession of the vernacular in the various services, the eucharist (Art. 54), the other sacraments and sacramentals (Art. 63a), the divine office (Art. 101), the sung liturgy (to the same extent as in the recited liturgy) (Art. 113).

(2) The promotion of studies necessary for the adaptations of the liturgy, whether those to be indicated in the revised liturgical books (Art. 38-39) or more profound adaptations that require pontifical consent (Art. 40), and the actual introduction or proposal of such adaptations.

(3) The establishment of an episcopal liturgical commission (Art. 44).

(4) The preparation of a particular or regional ritual after the publication of the revised Roman ritual (Art. 63b).

(5) The introduction of indigenous elements of religious initiation into the Christian ritual, at least in the so-called mission lands (Art. 65).

[11] *Ordo Baptismi Adultorum* . . . , Normae, n. 3, 5-6.
[12] *Motu Proprio*, n. IX; cf. F. R. McManus, "The Constitution on the Liturgy, Commentary, Part One," in *Worship* 38 (1964), pp. 358-61.

(6) The preparation of a rite for the celebration of matrimony "suited to the usages of place and people" (Art. 77).

(7) The adaptation of the liturgical year (Art. 107).

(8) The promotion of the practice of penance during Lent in ways "that are possible in our own times and in different regions" (Art. 110).

(9) The introduction of indigenous musical forms into the liturgy, especially in mission lands (Art. 119).

(10) The jurisdiction over the use of musical instruments other than the pipe organ in divine worship (Art. 120). This appears in the Constitution as a restriction of the right of individual local ordinaries (S.R.C., Instr. Sept. 3, 1958, n. 69).

(11) The adaptation of sacred furnishings and vestments, especially in their material and form, to the needs and customs of the region (Art. 128).

In one or other case, the above enumeration appears to impose an obligation rather than to describe a power, for example, in the promotion of the practice of penance. It would in fact be possible to dwell at length upon the new responsibilities of the territorial bodies of bishops, particularly with regard to liturgical education, promotion and participation (Art. 43-44). Beyond this, one particular question calls for brief comment.

In the case of the power possessed by the episcopal conferences over the introduction of the mother tongues into the liturgy (Art. 36, 3), and again in the case of the preparation of particular rituals (Art. 63b), the decrees of the territorial body require the confirmation of the Apostolic See.

The wording of the two pertinent articles was the subject of much controversy during the conciliar debate in the fall of 1962. In the schema of the Constitution, in the article which is numbered 36 in the final redaction, no power was acknowledged in the episcopal conferences in regard to the vernacular, only a right to make proposals to the Holy See—which is a meager right indeed.

Subsequently, the Conciliar Commission on the Liturgy submitted a new text of the article to the Fathers, in the form:

. . . *est competentis auctoritatis ecclesiasticae territorialis, de qua in art. 22, 2 . . . de usu et modo linguae vernaculae statuere, actis ab Apostolica Sede probatis seu confirmatis* (Art. 36, 3). The emendation was accepted by the Fathers by a vote of 2016 affirmative, 56 negative (Dec. 5, 1962).

The introduction of the word *statuere*—or rather its restoration, since the Pontifical Preparatory Commission had originally proposed it—indicates clearly the juridical power of the territorial authorities in this regard. Even the *Motu Proprio* of execution of the Constitution, which raised questions in its first version concerning the position of the episcopal conferences in relation to the Apostolic See, made the same point still more forcefully by the use of the expression, *ad legitima ferenda decreta* (*Motu Proprio,* n. X). It is a legislative power, in no way different from that of regional councils.

The other clause, requiring the confirmation of the decrees, was drawn with the greatest care, to indicate that the general approval expressed in the word *probatis* was of the kind expressed in the second word, *confirmatis.* This was the reason for the use of the conjunction *seu* rather than *vel,* a usage diligently retained in the final (and official) version of the January *Motu Proprio* and in rescripts of the new *Consilium* for the implementation of the Constitution. The word *seu* is thus properly translated into English as "that is" rather than as "or".

The sense of this confirmation is explained further by analogy with article 63b, dealing with the preparation of rituals by the territorial authorities. In this case the clause used is *actis ab Apostolica Sede recognitis.* The parallel demonstrates that the institute of canon 291, 1 (C.I.C.) is meant, whether this is called inspection, confirmation, review, ratification, or the like. The authentic explanation, offered to the Fathers by the Conciliar Commission, is a simple one: the laws in these cases are enacted by, and truly proceed from, the legislative authority of the territorial body of bishops; the laws receive an additional juridical and moral force from the subsequent confirmation of the Apostolic See, but their nature as episcopal law is not altered.

It would be possible to elaborate on this matter, especially as the Constitution draws upon the relationship of the Apostolic See to the legislation of provincial and plenary councils according to the code of canon law.[13] It is enough here to point out the juridical power vested in the episcopal conferences with regard to the liturgy, and to suggest that this may well be the first major step in the providential evolution of a new canonical institute, which will clarify the relationship of the chief bishop and the other bishops within the apostolic college.

[13] Cf. F. R. McManus, *art. cit.,* pp. 354-6.

# JOSEPH A. JUNGMANN, S.J.

Born November 16, 1889 in the South Tyrol,
Austria. He became a Jesuit and was ordained in
1913. He studied at the Universities of Innsbruck,
Munich and Vienna, and earned his doctorate in
theology in 1923 with the thesis, "Die Lehre von
der Gnade in den Katechetischen und Kerugma-
tischen Texten der ersten drei Jahrhunderte".
From 1934 to 1956 he taught pastoral theology
at the University of Innsbruck, and until 1963 was
editor-in-chief of *Zeitschrift für Katholische Theo-
logie*. His published works include *Die Stellung
Christi im liturgischen Gebet*, 1925; *Die lateinis-
chen Buszriten*, 1932; *Die Frohbotschaft und
unsere Glaubensverkundigung*, 1936; *Mass of the
Roman Rite*, 1950; *Katechetik*, 1953; *Early Liturgy to the Time of Gregory the Great*, 1959.

Joseph A. Jungmann, S.J./*Innsbruck, Austria*

# Liturgy, Devotions and the Bishop

It is a curious phenomenon that while in the Western Church the secular and regular clergy have a fully developed canonical office with carefully stipulated obligations, no such form of prayer is provided by the Church for the ordinary faithful, not even in the shape of official recommendation. The Church in China seems to be the only clear exception on this point.[1] This absence is the more striking when we look at the practice of the Church in the early centuries. In the oldest canonical work of the Church, the *Traditio Apostolica* of Hippolytus of Rome,[2] at least two of the forty-three paragraphs deal in detail with the prayer practice of the faithful, apart from those that treat of the eucharist. In our present canon law there are 2,414 canons of which, apart again from those treating of the eucharist or of religious, only canon 1259 really deals with the prayer of the faithful; paragraph 1 of this canon lays down: "Prayers and pious exercises in churches or oratories shall not be

[1] P. Brunner, *L'euchologe de la Mission de Chine* (Münster, 1964).
[2] In the new edition by B. Botte, *La Tradition Apostolique de Saint Hippolyte* (Münster, 1963), n. 88 (similar text, n. 35): *De tempore quo oportet orare,* and no. 42: *de signo crucis.*

permitted without the examination and express permission of the local Ordinary."

It is therefore taken for granted that, besides the liturgy and the clerical office, there are *pietatis exercitia* practiced by the people. But these receive only negative attention: the bishop's control must prevent abuses from creeping in, which might harm the faithful or be contrary to sound devotion.

The Instruction of the Congregation of Rites, of September 3, 1958, develops this canon in the same vein.[3] In order to clarify the scope of canon 1257, which reserves to the Holy See the right to regulate the form of worship, it gives a closer definition of *actio liturgica* as any act of worship that is performed by persons appointed for this purpose according to the rules contained in books approved by the Holy See. All other religious activities, whether inside the church or outside, are called *pia exercitia,* even when conducted by a priest.[4] Outside what is strictly liturgical this interpretation makes therefore no further distinctions among religious activities whether they concern individual pious practices, private pilgrimages, family prayers at home or parochial services announced and conducted by the appropriate priest.

This last instance concerns the various afternoon or evening services that have been held regularly for centuries in public churches, at least on Sundays and feast days. These clearly receive no particular attention. It is true that even though they are popular in many countries they mostly represent a random growth. The shape they took often originated from some private devotion or some nondescript prayer book. They have a habit of drifting toward the periphery—the veneration of some saint or some particular mystery. They show little interest in the phases of the liturgical year, particularly when they take the shape of novenas or monthly devotions. Devotion to St. Joseph can dominate the celebration of Lent throughout the

---

[3] *A.A.S.* 50 (1958), 633.
[4] *Ibid.:* "Ceterae actiones sacrae quae sive in ecclesia sive extra, sacerdote quoque praesente vel praeeunte, peraguntur, 'pia exercitia' appellantur."

whole of March; May devotions may flow over the Easter season without giving a thought to the risen Christ.

Yet, in his encyclical *Mediator Dei,* Pius XII treated these practices with approval and stressed their rightful place. He speaks there of pious practices (*pietatis exercitia*) that do not strictly belong to the liturgy but have special significance, and says that they can be taken as "somehow" falling within the scope of the liturgy. As examples he quotes the devotions to Mary in May and to the Sacred Heart in June, novenas, triduums and the Way of the Cross.[5] All these various devotions are recommended because they lead the Christian people to the sacrament of penance, to mass and communion, to meditation on the mysteries of our redemption and to imitation of the saints. He says that it is not necessary to adapt their structure to the rites of the liturgy though they ought to be inspired by the liturgy in such a way that they contain nothing unbecoming or unworthy of the house of God or contrary to the worship of God and sound piety.[6]

The Constitution on the Sacred Liturgy develops this line and thus introduces new perspectives into the field of a realistic pastoral care. The *pia exercitia* are first mentioned in article 13, and this in the broad traditional sense. They are strongly recommended with the obvious proviso that they do not go against the law of the Church, "above all when they are ordered by the Apostolic See". This clearly refers to such devotions as the rosary, the Way of the Cross and approved litanies. In the following paragraph, however, a distinction is made between these general *pia exercitia* and those *sacra exercitia* proper to individual churches, *i.e.,* the individual dioceses, and special dignity is attributed to these *sacra exercitia* if they are undertaken by mandate of the bishops according to customs or books lawfully approved. These *sacra exercitia* constitute therefore a smaller set of devotional practices that are distinguished within the domain of general and, until now, undifferentiated devotions. They are

[5] *A.A.S.* 39 (1947), 586.
[6] *Ibid.,* 587.

no longer treated as something foreign, something that developed outside the range of ecclesiastical guidance and laws, to be watched over by the Church more or less as the Church has to watch over forms of sport, recreation and entertainment in which the faithful indulge. They receive a more positive treatment as forms of worship that fall under the responsibility and direction of the bishop just as the liturgy in the strict sense generally falls under the responsibility and direction of the Holy See.

It is then an obvious conclusion when the Constitution lays down that these devotions should be in harmony with the liturgy and lead the faithful to it. The demand that they should "harmonize with the liturgical seasons" shows the weakness from which these practices so often suffer, as we know from experience.

The implications of article 13 are important. It starts by applying what was also laid down as a principle in article 22, 1, namely, that the right to regulate the liturgy belongs to the Holy See *and,* in the measure determined by the law, to the bishop. There is one field where this right of the bishop is of particular importance: the evening devotions. These have a peculiar history. The classical form of evening devotion is vespers or evensong. The ecclesiastical documents recommend this form of worship to the faithful again and again: Sunday vespers and Sunday mass are often mentioned in one breath. But it is equally well-known that vespers, at least where they are not celebrated in the vernacular,[7] are not popular with the ordinary faithful. Often popular devotions were introduced as a substitute. Yet, vespers are a religious service that goes back to the earliest years of the Church and still exists in all liturgical rites, whether of the East or of the West.

The Apostolic Constitutions compiled in the province of Antioch during the 4th century order the bishop to "gather the church together" daily in the evening and give special directions

---

[7] This has long been the case in Poland, for instance. Cf. J. Gülden, "Polnische Volksliturgie," in *Liturgisches Jahrbuch* 4 (1954), pp. 149-86, especially pp. 165-74.

for psalmody and prayer; this is followed by similar instructions
for the morning service.[8] At the same time, in the West St.
Hilary counted it a signal grace of God that the Church meets
"morning and evening for the singing of the psalms". [9] The regulation of matins[10] and vespers is a constantly recurring topic at
the synods of Gaul and Spain of the 6th and 7th centuries.[11] The
main preoccupation is here to establish a sound and uniform
way of psalm-singing everywhere. There is no lack of indications
that clearly show that the presence of the faithful was taken into
account.

The following centuries show a gradual decline of the morning
service while it becomes common to celebrate mass on weekdays.
Vespers, however, remain emphatically a part of the Church's
worship, particularly as evening service on Sundays and feast
days and the evening before these days. Through their greater
solemnity, vespers continue to stand out from the other hours
that have developed in the meantime from private practice to the
status of canonical hours. Yet, toward the end of the Middle
Ages even vespers lost their popularity. They were now fixed in
the form in which we still have them: with the verses of their
five psalms sung alternately, their versicles and antiphons, of old
adapted to a choir of monks or clerics, and in Latin. The faithful
saw themselves condemned to silence and were practically excluded.

This is why, toward the end of the Middle Ages, new ways of
worship, better adapted to the needs of the people, were organized, first in addition to vespers, later as a substitute. The *Salve
Regina,* which concluded vespers, was decked out with particular
solemnity (procession to the Lady altar, etc.) and further prayers were added. Thus arose the devotions that in many parts of

---

[8] VIII 35-39 (Funk I, 544-48).

[9] *In psalm 64,12* (CSEL 22, 244): *progressus Ecclesiae in matutinorum
et vespertinorum hymnorum delectationes maximum misericordiae Dei
signum est.*

[10] Matutinum = our present lauds.

[11] See J. A. Jungmann, *Liturgisches Erbe und pastorale Gegenwart*
(Innsbruck, 1960), pp. 175f., 180-2, 185f., 196f.

Germany are still known as *Salve* devotions and in France as *saluts*. In keeping with the peculiar eucharistic piety that dates from the 13th century, there developed also a eucharistic devotion at the end of vespers with the exposition of the blessed sacrament and its own hymns, called Benediction.[12]

Elsewhere other devotional services developed, built on the office, each with its own theme, and this was particularly popular with confraternities. These were composed, as was often the case in the Rhineland, of five successive sections, each starting with an invitation to prayer, including an *Our Father* and a *Hail Mary,* and closing with a collect. Or, again, they tried to make up a prayer service on the lines of a meditation or a religious instruction.[13] Or they might organize it on the basis of private devotions such as the rosary or the Way of the Cross.

This very variety in the solutions offered for the problem shows the uncertainty that prevailed; a clear principle was lacking. There was also a lack of sufficiently clear insight into the basic laws that ought to govern the Church's prayer and particularly the prayer of the congregation. Here we have the problem of how to organize the prayer of a community gathered round the priest, and therefore the prayer of the Church, just as in the days of the Fathers vespers represented congregational prayer, and just as, in a higher degree, vespers sung by a choir of clerics or monks constitutes their communal prayer.

It is truly the People of God of this parish or that community who is gathered here, and it is the parish priest or the priest delegated by him, and not just anybody, who leads the prayer, fully conscious that he acts according to the express wish of the bishop and that in this way congregational prayer is inserted into the prayer of the universal Church.

There will, of course, be a certain amount of freedom in the shaping of such a prayer service. It should not be tied to the

---

[12] P. Browe, "Die Entstehung der Sakramentsandachten," in *Jahrbuch für Liturgiewissenschaft* 7 (1927), pp. 83-103.

[13] Th. Schnitzler, "Messopferfeier und Nachmittagsandacht," in *Die Messe in der Glaubensverkündigung,* ed. F. X. Arnold and B. Fischer, 2nd ed. (Freiburg, 1953), pp. 354-63.

rules and regulations that govern today's official liturgy, as Pius XII said explicitly. It would even be wrong to press it into the framework of a part of the clerical office that involves quite different assumptions; yet there ought to be some basic laws, universally valid and derived from the very nature of a church gathering and of the Church's prayer. A first principle is found in article 13 where it points to the liturgical seasons and, by implication, to the great themes of the Christian revelation; instruction and meditation must, therefore, be based on the words of the Scriptures; this is in accordance with the good old tradition.

It is true that the early history of the office shows that in the beginning the monks were satisfied with the singing of psalms and hymns in order to praise God; but on Sundays and feast days, when the participation of the people had to be taken into account, the reading of the Scriptures was introduced. So it is still in the East.[14] And in the West we find that the Benedictine office, based on Roman tradition, had then, and still has, in every one of its canonical hours a final section corresponding to the structure of public worship and which begins with a scriptural reading called *Capitulum,* and then *via* some singing and the alternating prayer, called the *litania,* leads up to the collect.[15] In Rome that was an arrangement of long standing.

In the case of a full-size vigil this arrangement was repeated as often as necessary: six or twelve times. We still see this today in the readings on ember days and in the prophecies on the vigil of Easter: after the reading there follows singing, then we kneel for prayer and we conclude with a collect.

A second indication, pointing in the same direction, is contained in article 35, 4 of the Constitution. Here "Scripture services" are recommended on the vigils of the more solemn feasts, on some weekdays in Advent and Lent and on Sundays and feast days; this is precisely the sector that the evening devotions prin-

[14] R. Zerfass, "Die Rolle der Lesung im Stundengebet," in *Liturgisches Jahrbuch* 13 (1963).
[15] Cf. for details, J. A. Jungmann, "Wortgottesdienst," in *Die liturgische Feier,* 4th ed. (Regensburg, 1961).

cipally seek to cover. These Scripture services are given even higher significance since they are recommended as a substitute where no priest is available for the celebration of the eucharist.[16] Here again the authority of the bishop is emphasized: a deacon or "some other person authorized by the bishop" should preside over this service.

With all our profound respect for the classical form of vespers we shall have to look in the immediate future for suitable forms of vespers for the people, under the heading of *sacra exercitia*. These forms must show a certain latitude for the sake of variety. These *sacra exercitia* may be developed *secundum consuetudines* or *secundum libros legitime approbatos*. If we are to bring about a true renewal in this field, the faithful will need to be provided with a book. Important experiments have already been made in those dioceses where a diocesan prayer book has been in use for a considerable period, a prayer book that has been published under the auspices of the bishop and that is the pride and joy of the faithful.

[16] There are several projects in existence for such services without a priest; see, *e.g.*, J. Kellner, "Suggested Text for Sunday Service," in *Worship, the Life of the Missions* (Notre Dame, Ind., 1958), pp. 146-53.

———•••———

# JOSEPH GELINEAU, S.J.

Born in 1920 in Champ-sur-Layon, France, he became a Jesuit and studied at the Ecole César-Franck in Paris, the Faculté de théologie de Lyon/Fourvière, the Institut Catholique in Paris and the Pontifical Oriental Institute in Rome. He earned his doctorate in 1960 with the thesis, "Les formes liturgiques de la psalmodie dans les églises syriennes aux 4e-5e siècles". His activities are centered in the field of pastoral liturgy. One of his most important published works is *Chant et musique dans le culte chrétien,* 1962.

Joseph Gelineau, S.J. / *Paris, France*

# The Role of Sacred Music

The Lord's redeeming presence among his People, made manifest and operative particularly in the mystery of Christian worship, is not only active in the preaching of the Word and in the sacraments but in all liturgical actions as a whole. Christ "is present when the Church prays and sings, for he promised, 'Where two or three are gathered together in my name, there am I in the midst of them'" (Art. 7).

The chant of the liturgical assembly is therefore not for the faithful a purely exterior rite. Nor is it simply an exercise in the art of music. Nor can it be reduced to a mere psychological or social support for personal or communal prayer, a support to be used or dispensed with at will. It is one of those signs of "man's sanctification" and the Church's "public worship" (Art. 7) by which "the priestly office of Jesus Christ" is performed in the liturgy. Among other spiritual effects "it adds delight to prayer, fosters unity of minds, and confers greater solemnity upon the sacred rites" (Art. 112).

That is why liturgical chant is of great pastoral importance. As a privileged expression of man's religious life it is integrally embodied in the living faith of the Christian community. As a constitutive element of that "more noble form" of celebration which is called "solemn" (Art. 113), it becomes an integral part of the liturgical action (Art. 112). It can hardly be treated as a mere accessory in the exercise of a sound and liturgical-minded pastoral office.

Among the numerous pastoral problems to which the renewal of liturgical chant will give rise after the Council there are two that deserve special attention: (1) how to ensure continuity between new forms of liturgical singing and the liturgical tradition, and (2) what will be the place of the *scholae cantorum* or Church choirs in this development of congregational singing?

## I

### A Renewal in the Traditional Spirit

The liturgical Constitution has treated of sacred music in a special chapter (VI) because it concerns a ritual activity that is wholly *sui generis*. It assigns to this music its own *munus ministeriale,* insofar as it is "chant joined to words"; it then recalls some special norms that concern this song. These norms are traditional. In fact, the principles that concern this singing are loaded with pastoral consequences; they flow from the Constitution as a whole. This is particularly true of those principles that aim at the people's active participation—language and chant— because, apart from communion, singing is the principal means of actively and consciously participating in the sacred action.

On no other point perhaps does the renewal of the liturgy entail such important visible changes or run so many risks as in this domain of liturgical singing. Change of language, indeed, and the modification of texts used for certain hymns, psalms, readings or prayers, necessarily affect the music with which they were performed until now: in a good song words and melody correspond so intimately that one cannot change the language without changing the music.

When one translates the Scriptures or a liturgical text the

words change but the message remains the same and the linguistic communication, though necessarily modified since the sign and the signified correspond, remains similar. A change in music has no such safeguard. Music, by itself, has no notional content. The musical symbol is very weak in information, though very powerful in expressiveness. A change in music is, no doubt, less perilous because what it conveys is emotional rather than dogmatic. But faith, worship and devotion are not merely a matter of orthodox information; they imply a practical attitude and a weight of love with a considerable range of expression. Among these ways of expression sacred chant is one of the most important.

The necessary modification of the texts is bound to affect that "treasure of inestimable value, the musical tradition of the Church" (Art. 112), and through it, that particular religious attitude which the faithful found in it. This explains why the Church has to watch carefully that new flowering of hymns which the singing of the liturgy in various languages will entail. If the Church, therefore, points to the value of her musical tradition it is because we can only catch its spirit through the musical form that conveyed it. It deserves therefore a respect similar to what we have for the sacred texts, although on a totally different level.

It is clear, nevertheless, that the Council has left the door wide open for indigenous musical traditions (Art. 119). This point is essential to active participation since each culture expresses its religious and social life in its own music. But in sacred music one must distinguish between those melodies to be sung by the people or the choir and those belonging to the officiating clergy. If, for the former, one ought to look for a musical language most suitable to the faithful, should one not be guided as much as possible by the traditional melodies for use by celebrant or deacon, for readings from Scripture or verses of the psalms? Technically it is noteworthy that those formulas of the sung word are the most widely used parts of the ecclesiastical repertoire and, by their very nature (though with all necessary transpositions), most easily adapted to various languages. In this way the liturgy would retain a certain universality in its most invariable and sacred parts. Music has the privilege of being able to cross linguistic barriers, and so can be a powerful symbol of unity in worship.

## II

### THE TRUE FUNCTION OF THE CHOIR IN COMMUNAL SINGING

Why should the question of the choir's function be singled out here as the second point among all the problems raised by the Constitution on the Liturgy in connection with sacred music? Vatican Council II says nothing new about it: it is mentioned among the secondary liturgical services with which any well-organized congregation should be supplied (Art. 29); *scholae* are recommended, particularly in cathedrals (Art. 114), and so is a musical repertoire which takes account of small choirs as well as large ones (Art. 121). This is not very much. And these brief mentions are even relegated to the background insofar as active participation of all the faithful in the sacred action is constantly and insistently emphasized (*e.g.,* Art. 30, 33, 48, 54, 113, 114, 119, 121).

In comparison with previous documents, Vatican Council II clearly shows its pastoral preoccupation in its solicitude for the people's participation. In any case, nobody will deny that this insistence is opportune because in how many churches of the world is direct participation in the sacred chant of the liturgy still limited to the choir alone, even today? In these circumstances, would it not be contrary to the spirit of the Council to claim for the choir a part which should henceforth belong to the faithful?

It is true that the Council has decisively reminded us of what was clearly the practice in the days of St. John Chrysostom or St. Augustine, but gradually declined during the Middle Ages, namely, that the Church's prayer and praise included the voice of all its members and not merely that of a group of clergy or singers. On this point there is a notable difference between the *Motu Proprio* of St. Pius X and Vatican Council II. The former document, while laying down the principles of participation of the faithful in the liturgy and its sacred music, nevertheless confirmed a long-standing rule when it said: "Apart from the chant proper to the celebrant at the altar and the sacred ministers . . . all the rest of the liturgical chant belongs to the choir of levites" (*Tra le sollecitudini*, n. 30). Vatican Council II, on the contrary, mentions the sacred ministers and the people in its definition of the solemn and sung liturgy (Art. 113).

Nevertheless, to neglect the function of the choir would not be true to the spirit of the renewal of the liturgy. It would even be a mistake to consider as the ideal only a liturgical celebration where everybody would sing and the choir would be useless and superfluous. One ought indeed to remember (1) that, from the point of view of the liturgical celebration, the choir has a normal function in congregational singing; (2) that it plays an important part among the faithful; (3) that in the important development of hymnody in the near future it will be the choir's part to bear witness to the tradition and its spirit, not in order to produce musical fossils but to inspire a living practice.

1. The liturgical action is hierarchical and communal, as we are told in articles 26-32 of the Constitution. From this it follows that everyone must play his part, all of it and nothing else, according to his order, function and rank. The sacred chant of the solemn liturgy gives an excellent picture of this organic constitution of the celebrating congregation. When, in the sanctuary, the celebrant intercedes for the people or offers the sacrifice of praise, his voice is the most important and the most sacred. When the deacon calls the people to attention, sings the Gospel or suggests intentions to be prayed for, his voice is the voice of the servant of the whole congregation. The lector in charge of the sacred readings and the cantor singing the *Gradual* both lend their voices to the Church's unceasing proclamation of the Word of Life.

In the nave the people answer. They answer the greetings of

the celebrant and ratify his prayer; they answer the deacon when he sings the Gospel or the exhortations or the litanies; they answer the verses of the psalms sung by the cantor. But when the praise becomes more extensive or more powerful as in the *Gloria* hymn or the profession of faith in the *Credo;* when a more solemn chant accompanies the procession at the Introit or at Communion, the congregation will naturally seek the support of a choral group which will encourage and support, expand and discipline their voices. Such is the function of the choir: to assist the congregation singing in the nave.

2. The choir brings precious support to congregational singing and contributes in its own way to the festive character which the celebration demands of this musical performance.

The choir inspires and supports the singing of the congregation. Indeed, when the community of the faithful, only just come together from every direction, has not yet fully found itself in the Word and in prayer, and is still groping for its true harmony, the choir helps it to find its cohesion and oneness of mind. When the melody, perhaps forgotten or only half-known, begins to flag, the choir brings it to life again.

In longer and more developed pieces the choir can help by alternating with the congregation, *e.g.,* in the *Gloria* or the *Credo.* While the choir takes the verses or stanzas, the congregation will join in with an antiphon or a refrain, and so the choir ensures that harmonious rhythm in the performance of the common task by varying moments of action with moments of relaxation.

Lastly, because of its vocal qualifications, the choir provides an opportunity for festive or polyphonic singing which the people by themselves cannot manage but which contributes to the splendor of the celebration. If its singing truly aids the prayer of all, then the choir's function enriches the common action and all can actively participate in it.

3. If this is the choir's function according to the spirit of the Constitution on the Liturgy, one has to admit that, in spite of its

reticence on the subject, the Constitution introduces and demands much that is new in relation to established uses. Often, indeed, the choir's function has been to provide a substitute for the silent congregation. Its repertoire has frequently been based on the absence of the voice of the congregation, as in the parts of the *Kyriale*. That should no longer happen (Art. 114, 28 and 30). The spirit of the liturgical renewal in no way demands the suppression or the silence of the choir. On the contrary, it takes the choir for granted and assesses its liturgical value on its connection with the celebration itself. But in many cases the Constitution calls for a renewal and a conversion of the choir system: a renewal through a repertoire that "encourages the active participation of the whole congregation of the faithful" (Art. 121); and its conversion in a spirit that pays more attention to its part in the liturgy than to the purely technical or aesthetic prestige of its performances.

Finally, it should be added that the liturgical renewal, calling for new creativeness in every language, has given the choir a mission: transmitting to the newly restored congregational singing that true spirit contained in "the inestimable treasure of the Church's musical tradition" (Art. 112). In the choir it is easier to let oneself be permeated by the pure sources of the Church's sacred music and to transmit to the people its spiritual substance. It is the choir's part to bear witness to it, to create the taste for it and to make its spirit pervade all.

For this, however, two conditions are required. The first is to know how to select compositions from the past which truly agree with the liturgy as envisaged by Vatican Council II. They are numerous, but, all the same, the choice will be limited to only a part—important and basic—of plainsong and a much smaller portion of other repertoires. The second condition is that the choir must not defend an aesthetic repertoire and prefer artistic compositions to the sacred action, but rather ensure continuity in an evolution in which the same spirit will sing in other tongues, with other voices and with tunes both old and new.

# GODFREY DIEKMANN, O.S.B.

Born in 1908 in Roscoe, Minnesota, U.S.A. He
became a Benedictine, and was ordained June 28,
1931. He studied at the Collegio di Sant' Anselmo
in Rome and at the liturgical institute in Maria
Laach, Germany, and earned his doctorate in
theology with the thesis, "De imagine Dei in
homine secundum Tertulliani Scripta". He is
professor of patrology at St. John's Seminary,
and professor of theology at St. John's University, both in Collegeville, Minnesota. His interests
and activities are mainly in the liturgical field.
He is editor of *Worship*, a member of the Executive Board of the National Liturgical Conference,
a *peritus* at Vatican Council II and a consultor to
the Post-Conciliar Liturgical Commission.

Godfrey Diekmann, O.S.B./*Collegeville, Minn., U.S.A.*

# The Place of Liturgical Worship

Whoever expected to find anything like a practical blueprint of the liturgical arrangement of the church in Chapter VII of the Constitution on the Sacred Liturgy, which deals with "Sacred Art and Sacred Furnishings", will have been seriously disillusioned. In fact, no single detailed directive is offered. Instead article 124 merely states the general principle that "when churches are to be built, great care should be taken that they be suitable for the celebration of liturgical services and for the active participation of the faithful". And article 128 asks for an early revision of the existing legislation which governs "the worthy and well-planned construction of sacred buildings", mentions specifically the problems of altar, tabernacle and baptistry which are to be solved, and empowers the territorial bodies of bishops to adapt the legislation to the rules and customs of their respective regions in accordance with the norm established in article 22.

At first sight, it would therefore seem premature, if not presumptuous, to venture an essay on the liturgical arrangements of the church in the light of the Constitution. However, the same article 128 stipulates that the new regulations are to be brought into harmony with "the reformed liturgy", that is, the principles enunciated in this Constitution about the nature and the celebration of community worship. Our problem is not primarily one of style, but of the data of faith. It is one of applying the *altiora principia,* which Pope John had instructed the Pontifical Preparatory Liturgical Commission to draw up in its draft document, and which have been substantially embodied in the Constitution, to the specific questions relating to the disposition of space and liturgical furnishings. The implementation of Chapter VII by the Postconciliar Liturgical Commission will be in the nature of conclusions drawn from Chapters I to V, as well as from the principles and fresh insights gained from the Council's discussions about such related topics as those of the Church and the respective role of the hierarchy and the laity.

In terms of the history of the liturgical movement, this means that the circle has come full turn. For it is generally admitted that the pastoral liturgical renewal of today had its effective beginning in a talk by Dom Lambert Beauduin at a national Belgian Catholic convention in 1909, a talk which was considered irrelevant to the purpose of the congress by the organizers, and was finally allowed to be delivered under the auspices of the "Art and Archeology" section. Similarly, the principle of "active and intelligent participation", which proved such a decisive factor in promoting the liturgical movement during its nearly forty years of desert wandering, derived from a *Motu Proprio* dealing with music: St. Pius X's *Tra le sollecitudine* of November 22, 1903. And even as recently as 1958, the important Instruction of the Sacred Congregation of Rites still gave priority to the art of music in its title, "On Sacred Music and the Sacred Liturgy". The liturgy's debt to "art and archeology" has been paid. The Constitution firmly puts first things first.

Our essay will therefore attempt above all to draw what seem to be reasonable deductions from the *altiora principia* contained in the Constitution, supplemented where necessary by the pertinent decisions on the nature of the Church that have taken place on the Council floor. It goes without saying that our concrete suggestions can sometimes be only tentative, awaiting confirmation or correction by the norms to be issued by the Postconciliar Commission on the Liturgy. Fortunately, however, there already exists a preview of the probable content of at least some of those norms in an *Appendix* made available to the Fathers of the Council before their vote on Chapter VII, containing more detailed declarations on article 128. The anticipatory significance of this *Appendix,* drawn up by the Liturgical Preparatory Commission, is all the greater because many of the persons responsible for its composition are now actively engaged in the Postconciliar Commission. It therefore represents an invaluable hint of "the shape of things to come".[1] In the following, we shall refer to it simply as the *Appendix.*

I

THE CHURCH IS THE PEOPLE OF GOD, THE SACRAMENT OF UNITY

In the first principle of reform drawn from the nature of the liturgy itself, the Constitution declares that "liturgical services are not private functions, but are celebrations of the Church, which is the 'sacrament of unity', namely, the holy people united and ordered under their bishops. Therefore liturgical services pertain to the whole body of the Church; they manifest it and have effects upon it" (Art. 26).

One of the most significant achievements of the second session of the Council was the vote to revise the order of chapters in the proposed schema *De Ecclesia.* Instead of treating first of Christ, then of the hierarchy, and thirdly of the laity, the new schema presented first Christ, second the entire *populus Dei,* and then only the articulation of this People of God into the hierarchical priesthood and the faithful to whom it ministers. A telling criti-

---

[1] An English translation was published in the February 1964 issue of *Liturgical Arts,* pp. 42-43, and a German version, not however identified as such, appears in *Die konstitution du zweiten vatikanischen konzils über die heilege Liturgie, Lebendiger Gottendienst 5/6,* by Emil J. Lingeling (Münster, 1964), pp. 243-6.

cism against the original sequence was the reminder to the Fathers of the Council that it failed to correspond to the more scripturally accurate ecclesiology that they had already approved in the schema "On the Sacred Liturgy".

It was Pius XII, in *Mediator Dei,* who had made current the descriptive definition of the liturgy as "the public worship which our redeemer, the head of the Church, offers to the heavenly Father and which the community of Christ's faithful pays to the founder, and through him to the eternal Father; briefly it is the whole public worship of the Mystical Body of Jesus Christ, head and members" (*A.A.S.* 39 [1947] pp. 528-9). The liturgy is the exercise of the priestly office of Christ, continued through the ages in and by his Body, which is the Church, the People of God.

The Constitution, especially in articles 2, 7, 26, and 41-42, adopts and further clarifies the statements of *Mediator Dei* about the Church as a community of worship. The liturgy is the preeminent epiphany of the Church, whereby its members are built into a holy temple of the Lord, a dwelling-place for God in the Spirit. It is the action of Christ the priest and of his Body which is the Church. The Church is God's holy People offering the same eucharist at which presides the bishop or his ordained representative.

Writing against the Gnostics, the early Apologists had insisted that we Christians have neither temple nor sacrifice nor altar. Thus Tertullian: "Temples and tombs, we detest both equally; we know neither kind of altar . . . we offer no sacrifice" (*De Spectaculis* 13). No physical walls are needed to build our true temple, no massive stone constitutes our altar. "God does not dwell in temples built by hands," Paul had told the Athenians (Acts 17,24). The "worship in spirit and in truth" of which Christ spoke to the Samaritan woman (John 4,23) took place in Christ's own sacred Body; it is the temple in whom God dwells (John 2,19-21), the altar on which the perfect sacrifice is offered, at which sinful man encounters his heavenly Father to be reconciled and united with him. In the new Dispensation, the temple of true worship is a person; the person of Christ, who continues after his ascension to dwell in his Body, the Church, thereby transforming it likewise into a spiritual house of which the members are the living stones (Eph. 2,20-22; 1 Pet. 2,5). The early Christian community, meeting together for Sunday worship, were vividly aware of Christ in their midst; Paul and Peter in their letters merely put into words the shared eucharistic experience of the holy People of God, itself constituting the *ecclesia*.

It was only several generations later that the term *ecclesia* began also to be applied to the room or building in which the living *ecclesia* met for worship. But the priority of emphasis remained on the community of persons, on the assembly of God's family under the leadership of its bishop, gathered to hear God's Word, to celebrate with thanksgiving the memorial of Christ's saving death and resurrection and to receive its fruits. The material *ecclesia* was of importance only inasmuch as it offered a fixed locale for the assembly, and by its physical arrangement of space and furnishings contributed to the proper functioning of the worshiping community. Later centuries were to attach symbolic significance to the church building: God's fortress in Romanesque times, his royal audience hall in the period of the Baroque. And attaching such adventitious meanings to the physical structure has remained a temptation to which architects have continued to succumb to our own day, not infrequently with disastrous results in terms of the primary purpose of the building, which is simply to supply a space so planned that the living *ecclesia* may therein aptly function at its highest and most important potential. The church building can be called genuinely symbolical only if, by the arrangement of its parts, it makes clear how the *ecclesia* which is the People of God, clergy and faithful, fulfill the various and interrelated actions that constitute its *raison d'être*.

The physical *ecclesia* must be an expression of the worshiping Church, the "sacrament of unity", such as it exists in the world of today in order to transform it.

And therefore, while it is true, as the Constitution declares in article 112, that among the arts music enjoys preeminence because "it forms a necessary or integral part of the solemn liturgy", the task of the architect is in one respect even more important. For bad music can be eliminated and changed for better. But a church building and its physical arrangements have a disconcerting permanence. And they do play a decisive role in creating a true community of worshipers. Liturgical action teaches the mystery of Christ's priestly action in the present at its deepest and most formative level. But it is self-defeating to exhort the faithful to full participation in the sacred mysteries in a church which makes it practically impossible for them to do so. Nor need one think, in this context, only of the extreme instances of the medieval rood-screen, or the high walls that still separate the faithful from both sanctuary and the greater part of the nave in, for instance, many Spanish and Mexican cathedrals. As a modern author has stated:

> If you are going to build a church
> you are going to create a thing which speaks.
> It will speak of meanings, and of values,
> and it will go on speaking.
> And if it speaks of the wrong values
> it will go on destroying.[2]

It may be argued with plausibility that the liturgical arrangements of space in the ancient basilicas have been the best yet devised, due no doubt to the biblical and patristic understanding of the Church and its liturgical life that characterized that era. But we now enjoy technical advances in architecture and engineering then unknown, which make it possible to achieve even better solutions. This, coupled with the contemporary synthesis of biblical, ecclesiological and liturgical insights that has found such admirable expression in the Constitution, opens a greater

---

[2] Robert Maguire, "Meaning and Understanding," in *Towards a Church Architecture,* edited by Peter Hammond (London, 1962), p. 66.

opportunity and imposes a more urgent responsibility upon planners of church buildings than ever before. To be authentically contemporary is not only a matter of using modern methods or materials of construction honestly, though this is not negligible; rather it means to mirror and facilitate the new self-realization of the *ecclesia* in her primary privilege and duty of common worship. For the church building is the "house of God" (a term, by the way, used only once in the entire Constitution: in article 126) chiefly insofar as therein the living house of God carries out its worship tasks, and thereby becomes God's dwelling-place ever more fully. *Ecclesia,* in a word, signifies a Person and persons engaged in due confrontation, dialogue and unifying action, before it can aptly signify a thing plus the objects contained therein.

The recent history of the liturgical movement strikingly bears this out. It was in army and war-prison camps—when reduced to the bare essentials of worship, in a personal encounter of priest and lay soldiers stripped of all external props—that the reality of the liturgy and the meaning of Church were discovered anew by thousands. To this discovery the pastoral-liturgical renewal of the postwar years largely owes its dynamism. It would be tragic irony if this new vitality were to be dimmed by the very building and space arrangements whose only reason for existence is to foster and increase it. Lest this happen, perhaps it will often be desirable for some time to come to limit the building and arrangements to the essentials in order to recapture the experience of a living community for our people who have lost it or have become distracted, confused and absorbed by the peripheral.

Actually, the principles enunciated by the Constitution had already been stated to a surprisingly large extent in Pius XII's *Mediator Dei.* The significant difference, however, lies precisely in the Constitution's stress on this personal-encounter dimension of the liturgy; that is, on its concretely pastoral approach, in contradistinction to the more generally theological concern of *Mediator Dei.*

The *ecclesia,* as worshiping People of God, most effectively manifesting the infinite mystery of the Church, ranks among the *altiora principia* of the Constitution.

### (1) *The Local Worshiping Assembly Is the Church*

Pius XII's statement in *Mediator Dei* on the "presence" of Christ in every liturgical action (*A.A.S., Loc. cit.,* p. 528) probably had more theological impact than anything else in that document. We had become so accustomed to speak of Christ's "Real Presence" in the eucharist that unwittingly we considered his other modes of presence as somehow unreal or figurative. Article 7 of the Constitution similarly represents a theological high point, but also an advance over the parallel text in *Mediator Dei* in two important points: Christ's presence in his scriptural word (about this, later), and his presence in the local worshiping community. Pius XII had indeed cited Matthew 18,20: "Where two or three are gathered in my name, there I am in the midst of them." But it was in order to include the divine office among the chief liturgical actions that involve Christ's presence. The Constitution, however, true to its pastoral emphasis, quotes the passage to stress the presence itself in the local worshiping *ecclesia.* This is born out by articles 41-42, another of the most theologically and pastorally pregnant statements of the Constitution. The local worshiping community, gathered around the bishop or around the pastor of a parish especially in the celebration of the eucharist, is the preeminent epiphany of the Church. The parish at worship in some manner represents the visible Church throughout the world.

The Constitution thereby authoritatively puts its stamp of approval on "the theology of the assembly" which, based on scriptural and patristic emphases, has played such a prominent role in liturgical writings in recent years. The local assembly (let us call it, for convenience sake, the parish) is more than a geographical or administrative division of the universal Church. It is "in some manner" that Church itself; and it had its historical origins, as Pius XII wrote to the Canadian Social Action Week on August 14, 1953, precisely in order that the members of the Church might, by worshiping together, experience community more fully and normally.

And while the Council and the Constitution have opted for the term "People of God", the liturgy itself gives an even more intimately personal interpretation of this "People" by calling it *"familia"*, e.g., in many collects, and in the *Hanc igitur* prayer of the canon. We are *famuli Dei,* and never so much as when we gather with the other members of our family at the family sacrificial meal. In fact, a good case could be made for the thesis that both Scripture and Tradition, up to and including St. Thomas Aquinas, stress fellowship (*koinonía*), or what might be called the horizontal dimension of the eucharistic action, as much if not more than its purpose of uniting us to the Father, that is, its vertical dimension. Thomas summarizes it in his classic statement: *Res huius sacramenti est unitas mystici corporis* (*Summa Theol.* III, 73,3).

If the church building has as its primary purpose to create a suitable space for the local worshiping community, it follows that the primary objective in the arrangement of space must be the common experience of community, or better, of family, above all in the eucharistic action. It is the one Body of Christ, filled with Christ's own Spirit, that constitutes God's "household" (Eph. 2,20). Unity precedes distinction of parts, and the latter is possible only on the basis of the former. And since this unity is one of persons, though with diversity of roles, the church spaces should not exceed a personal, human scale. Cathedral or pilgrimage churches may perforce have to be exceptions; but the parish church, if it is not to frustrate its chief function, must normally have a human dimension of size in which the person is not swallowed up in an anonymous mass. It is cynicism to speak of a community or of a family, in which the experience of personal encounter with both head and fellow members of the body is *a priori* ruled out or rendered next to impossible.

This involves, of course, what is undoubtedly the most grievous pastoral problem today: the huge city parish. For while it is true that parishes are of ecclesiastical institution, the *raison d'être* of a parish, that a pastor may *know* and serve his flock, is divine law clearly indicated by Christ. Small wonder that an old and wise bishop of a metropolis remarked some years ago: "The chief cause of leakage in the Church is mass every hour on the hour." When the industrial assembly-belt system substitutes for assembly, all talk about the eucharist creating a family is largely wasted breath. Whatever the solution, we can at least begin to meet the problem by building churches in human scale, that is to say, buildings that serve the community rather than grandiose "monuments to God's glory".

Liturgically minded pastors in various countries seem to have arrived at a consensus that this means a maximum of 600 to 700 places for the faithful. Or, as the *Richtlinien* of the German bishops (cf. bibliography) state: "There is an ideal maximum for the size of any church: the priest at the altar must be clearly seen and heard in the farthest pew without the use of technical aids, and it must be possible to give communion to everyone present without disrupting the celebration of the mass" (n.19). There have, however, been several recent experiments, with reasonable success, of increasing the size to about a thousand, by means of a cantilevered balcony. In any event, the sense of family, of personal confrontation and common human action, must predominate in the fixation of architectural spaces in order that "the Christian people be enabled . . . to take part in the sacred rites fully, actively, *and as befits a community*" (Art. 21). Sunday afternoon masses and an extension of the permission already granted to some dioceses of Saturday afternoon and evening masses fulfilling the Sunday obligation will help to relieve the pressure that has all too often in the past resulted in a "filling-station" approach to liturgical worship, and found expression in parish church buildings vying in monumentality with cathedrals.

To achieve a building which, in the spatial organization of personal relationships, truly serves the community, the architect must be furnished a liturgical brief, or program, not only of the general principles of worship and the purposes of a church, but a particular brief of this specific community of worship. His client, however, is not merely the pastor, assisted by members of the diocesan art commission, together with a competent sociologist, acoustical expert and artist; the client is the parish family, presided over by a spiritual father. The collaboration of the parish, a factual and not only nominal plus financial collaboration, could and should be a uniquely precious opportunity of liturgical formation. All are called upon by St. Paul to "build up the Body of Christ", all are "living stones" in this structure. Selecting a truly representative parish committee, keeping all informed about the planning and its why's and wherefore's, and establishing an effective channel through which questions can be asked and suggestions offered, would seem minimum requirements to achieve a true home for God's holy People.

## (2) *The Local Ecclesia Represents the Universal Church*

In its spatial arrangements, the church images the worshiping *ecclesia* in action, insofar as it can be called a symbol or sacramental sign of the mystery of the Church. But a purely practical structure and arrangement, designed solely with the local *ecclesia* in mind, would be a misleading symbol: for the mystery of the Church is the mystery of God's holy People, with its roots in the Old Testament, its realization in the Body of Christ, historical and mystical, and its fulfillment at the Parousia. "The parish in some manner represents the visible Church constituted throughout the world" (Art. 42). Only if the church building and its arrangements inspire contemplation of this total mystery of the Church can it be called truly functional. It must serve the local community by helping it discover also its cosmic dimension, by widening its vision to include diocese, Church and world. Parochialism is the negation of genuine parish spirit. The eucharistic celebration must again inspire a charity like that of Paul, admonishing his new congregations to "collections" (the word has liturgical connotations) for the Church of Jerusalem, or like that of Justin, who in his famous description of the mass includes a collection for "all who are in need" as an integral component of the service (*Apology* I, 67).

In our age of triumphant secularism, this missionary obligation of every local *ecclesia* needs expression more than ever before. Perhaps it is time we break away from the too literal interpretation of the church building as a "space enclosed", by lower-
ing the deep-chasm (or ghetto) walls which at best inspire eschatological rather than incarnational devotion, and also by dis-
cretely opening a few windows to the world outside (even
though this be a quiet, cloistral space), as Pope John hoped
might happen to the universal Church through the Council. The
relationship to the bishop and cathedral church could be intimated by a vigil light before the ambry for oils, the latter of a
size and in a location not unworthy of its sacred contents.

But the rite of the consecration of a church suggests the most
effective architectural means of counteracting parochial self-cen-
teredness. This local *ecclesia,* too, is built on Christ as the chief
cornerstone (the altar), and upon the foundation of the apostles
(the consecration crosses). Giving these crosses such visual and
structural prominence that all who enter the building are immediately aware of them can be an eloquent lesson in catholicity.
This is the case, for instance, in the restored cathedral of Cuer-
navaca in Mexico: the crosses are of rough stone, projecting
boldly from the wall, and at the side of each is a smaller symbol
in stone of the respective apostle. The impact is memorable.
Such crosses could be made a structural part of the building even
when there is no immediate prospect of actual consecration. This
would entail, moreover, placing the customary stations of the
cross elsewhere, where they would not obscure or conflict with
the far more important consecration crosses.

### (3) *Distribution of Roles*

"In liturgical celebrations each person, minister or layman, in
the discharge of his office should do all of, but only, those parts
which pertain to his office by the nature of the rite and the principles of the liturgy" (Art. 28).

Here undoubtedly we have another of the *altiora principia* of history-making importance. The new Holy Week Ordo had initiated the process of eliminating duplications of function in regard to the readings; the September 1958 Instruction further prepared the ground by speaking of some parts of the mass which "of their nature" belong to the congregation, but had failed to draw the full practical consequences. The Constitution, in a clear-cut reversal of a thousand and more years' process of clericalizing the liturgy, restored the principle of distribution of roles according to office. The entire holy "People of God" are again to join in the eucharist according to their respective rank, as Clement of Rome had exhorted the Corinthians at the turn of the 1st century (*To the Corinthians,* I, 40-41), and as Paul, writing to the same audience earlier, had intimated by speaking of the distribution of gifts and functions immediately after his description of the eucharistic celebration (1 Cor. 12).

Nor is this principle of distribution of roles restricted to the mass. The entire liturgy is the common action of the People of God, under the leadership of their ministerial priests. Hence article 31 states the general norm that the "revised liturgical books must carefully attend to the provision of rubrics also for the parts that belong to the faithful".

The basic distinction of roles, by divine institution, is of course that of ministers (*nos servi tui*) and the congregation (*sed et plebs tua sancta*). The Church as the Body of Christ has head and members. From earliest times, therefore, in all liturgies, there has been a zone for the clergy and another for the laity: "sanctuary" and "nave". But these two zones are complementary rather than divisive; the nave is not a spatial adjunct to the sanctuary, but with it forms one organically united place of worship; they are areas for mutually related action of persons. Thus the famous description of an early church building in the *Constitutiones Apostolorum* (ii, 57) dating from the late 4th century, speaks of the placing of ministers and laity without even mentioning the location of the altar. Only a humble meditation on the respective relations of the ministers and the faithful whom they serve in the common action of the mass as well as other liturgical rites can result in a disposition of space that promotes participation "as befits a community".

(a) *Celebrant:* The 1958 Instruction had already stated: "The priest celebrant *presides* over the entire liturgical service" (n. 92). Yet, present rubrics, with some exceptions in the new Holy Week Ordo, provide only for his presiding within the sanctuary, at the altar. Thus, for instance, the 1960 new Code of Rubrics merely repeats the *Rubricae generales* of the Missal of Pius V, that in a solemn or sung mass "the celebrant may sit . . . at the epistle side, near the altar, while the *Kyrie, Gloria,* sequence and *Credo* are being sung" (n. 523). His service of the altar is thereby indicated, to the total neglect of his relation of presidency over the faithful.

The Constitution reiterates the presidential role of the celebrant (*e.g.,* articles 33, 41, 42) and in addition insistently underscores the ministerial nature of his priesthood. The headship of the Christian community, after the example of Christ, is an authority rooted in the charity of service, not in domination: *Regnavit a ligno Deus*—The cross was God's throne. This emphasis on the ministerial relation of the clergy to the faithful, coupled with the high probability of the Service of the Word taking place not at the altar but at the lectern and priest's bench (sedile), and finally the projected new rite of concelebration—all these factors will influence the disposition of liturgical space.

The location of the sanctuary at the head of the nave and its greater elevation are functionally and therefore symbolically sound. Yet the elevation should be moderate to facilitate sight and hearing and dialogue, suggesting the leadership of ministry rather than "lording it over one's charges" (1 Pet. 5,3). Its floor-plan should logically begin with consideration, not of the altar, as has been largely customary in the recent history of the liturgical movement, but with thought of the celebrant and ministers, *i.e.,* with persons, *and* their relation to the faithful at the several places at which they serve: altar, sedile, and lectern.

Thus article 7 significantly lists "in the person of his minister" first among the various manners of Christ's high-priestly "presence" in liturgical action. And the *Appendix* speaks "Of the Place of Those who Preside" (n. 2) before treating of "The Main Altar" (n. 3). Nor is it irrelevant to remember that *"cathedra"*, the place of the presiding bishop, is the root word of "cathedral".

Doubtless, the altar is the place of the most important action for the celebrant. But there is little likelihood that this fact will be neglected in the planning. What requires new thought is the placing of the sedile and lectern, related organically and serviceably to both altar and congregation. The *Appendix* suggests that the sedile be placed at the head of the assembly, in the middle of the apse, not only in cathedrals but also in parish churches, in the latter case avoiding any semblance of throne (n. 2). For the priest presides in the name of the bishop. If this proves unfeasible, a position on the "Epistle side" of the sanctuary near the apse, with the bench turned wholly or diagonally toward the faithful, would seem second-best. The sedile is more than a piece of furniture, like the credence table, that happens to be needed at certain times of the mass. It will likely be the normal place of the priest's presidency during the Service of the Word, for delivering the homily, and perhaps often for proclaiming the Gospel. Visual and acoustical requirements must therefore be met.

The lectern will be considered later. But perhaps it might here be suggested that constructing altar, sedile and lectern of the same material could be didactically effective in symbolizing their organic mutual relationship.

The sanctuary should be ample enough to allow for reasonably convincing entrance as well as Gospel "processions". Cathedral sanctuaries evidently have their own special requirements, *e.g.*, for ordination services, the blessing of oils, the concelebration of larger numbers. But in the average parish church, concelebration will merely entail sufficient space near the sedile for several priests, during the Service of the Word, who will then proceed to and surround the altar during the eucharistic service.

The amplitude of the sanctuary space must be disciplined by normal needs, which however presuppose a solemn mass rather than a low mass as a norm. This would usually be sufficient also to meet the growing custom of ordaining a priest in his home parish; for it seems certain that for such cases a radical simplification of the pontifical rites will be permitted. Any spaciousness beyond those needs could only result in ceremoniousness of ritual, perpetuate an impression of clericalism and might even lead the irreverent to speak of their church as suffering from hydrocephalus.

In the context of ministerial priesthood, a sacristy near the entrance of the church, to allow the priest to meet and mingle with his people after mass, recommends itself: it would help to overcome some of the disadvantages of the impersonal large city parish and also facilitate the full entrance procession. The experiment, where tried, seems to have enthusiastic supporters. An auxiliary sacristy, off the sanctuary, would still however be necessary, at least for storage purposes. Moreover, in the usual arrangement in which a door leads from sanctuary to sacristy, another door from the sacristy directly into the nave is now more than ever called for, not only that the faithful will not have to traverse the sanctuary, but especially in view of the *Introit* procession.

(b) *Choir:* "Members of the *schola cantorum* exercise a genuine liturgical function" (Art. 29). Such *scholae* "must be diligently promoted, especially in cathedral churches; *but* bishops and other pastors of souls must be at pains to insure that, whenever the sacred action is to be celebrated with song, the whole body of the faithful may be able to contribute that active participation which is rightly theirs" (Art. 114).

The choir, accordingly, has an organic relation to both sanctuary and nave. It represents the congregation, but also helps it to perform its worship in song more worthily. As a matter of fact, however, the tale of the location of the choir in a church resembles an historical tragedy on the theme of popular participation, with the final act, taking place in the rear balcony, the saddest of all. Its optimum placement presents undoubted problems. Negatively, it is easy enough to condemn the rear balcony; and also, less violently, a screened-off place at the head of the apse, for in the latter instance, this functionally important group of persons in liturgical action would be withdrawn from the "presidency" of the celebrant. Since it is a link between clergy and congregation, it would seem that it belongs at the head of the congregation, not too far removed from the latter in whose name it functions, whom it assists, and for whom it sometimes supplies. And since the choir director often has to direct the people as well, a position at the "Epistle side" of the sanctuary, where the director would have easy access to the commentator's stand, appears preferable. The increasing toleration of instrumentalists, moreover, argues not only for more space, but also for a discreet screen to avoid inevitable distraction. This location would likewise answer the concern of the *Appendix* that choir members can readily approach the communion table (n. 8).

(c) *Commentator:* The commentator's "genuine liturgical function" is recalled in article 29, and in article 35, 3 there is mention of the priest "or proper minister" who provides brief directives during the various rites. His role is of its nature "diaconal"; yet because no longer exercised normally in the Western Church by ordained deacons, but by a lay person, his functionally correct place is not the lectern or ambo, but the "presanctuary" area connecting clergy and laity zones. It is especially important that provision be made for his being heard easily, for he is to use "a moderate tone of voice" (1958 Instruction, n. 96c), in order not to call attention to himself; and again in the interest of unobtrusiveness, since the proper location of the ambo is on the "Gospel side", the commentator might fittingly balance things by standing to the far right on the "Epistle side".

When the liturgical reform will give us more easily comprehensible rites "which do not require much explanation" (Art. 34), and especially if a functional diaconate will be restored, the role of the commentator, however needful now, may again disappear. There will probably be few laments.

(d) *The Congregation:* It is not the sanctuary alone which is a holy place, with nave attached by way of forecourt. The entire holy People of God, head and body, constitute the spiritual house, the holy priesthood, to offer spiritual sacrifices to God through Jesus Christ. The "body" of this spiritual house is therefore (1) a community, (2) of persons, (3) assembled to see and listen, to respond and to join in the common worship action together with the ministers according to their rank.

To experience community, a certain spatial cohesion is imperative. A desire to bring the people closer to the altar has often resulted in a reprehensible division of the congregation itself, *e.g.,* in nave and deep transepts. A means has thereby been exalted at the expense of the very purpose of the liturgy and particularly of the eucharist, namely, "a more perfect union with God *and with each other*" (Art. 48). Common prayer, song and acclamations likewise, demand spatial cohesiveness of participants. Christian community further requires, negatively, rejection of privileged place for individuals based on reasons of social prestige (Art. 32), and positively, a sensitive concern for the needs of the ailing members. Hence special hearing aids should be available not only in the confessionals but also in some pews; and a wide side-aisle or pre-sanctuary space, close to the communion table for the accommodation of those in wheel chairs. (Where are these members of the Christian community on an average Sunday? A glance at a Sunday congregation might lead one to suspect we have reached a Utopia of physical fitness.)

One of the most striking *altiora principia* of the Constitution is the constant stressing of the personal faith-dimension demanded by liturgical actions. The People of God is constituted of persons, and community worship is acceptable to God only to the degree of personal faith-involvement of the worshipers. Spatially, therefore, the body of worshipers should be sufficiently articulated by aisles and not-too-lengthy pews, to avoid any impression of mere multitude in which the person is no more than a cipher. Even at the multiplication of the loaves and fishes, a foreshadowing of the eucharistic meal, Christ had commanded that the crowd be seated by fifties and hundreds! The plea for a "human scale" in the church building, mentioned earlier, also has relevance in this context.

If the congregation were assembled merely to see and listen, the spatial requirements could conceivably be met by eliminating obstructing pillars and then furnishing opera glasses and a perfect loud-speaking system. But the era of "mute spectators" is, please God, drawing to a close. The Constitution more urgently than any previous official directive calls for action by the faithful, such as befits "the chosen race, the royal priesthood, the holy nation" (*e.g.*, Arts. 14, 21, 30, 33, 36, 41, 42). By right of baptism, they share in the holy rites performed in their name by the priestly minister, at altar, ambo and sedile. Spacious aisles are requisite for processions, particularly those of entrance and communion. While the offertory procession may, in realistic practice, often prove no more than a nostalgic memory, the offertory collection, which is a significant liturgical action, postulates short enough pews so that it can take place expeditiously, without extending into the canon of the mass. Shorter and amply spaced pews are likewise conducive to mutual charity at the time of going to receive the sacrament of love.

The chief spatial objective, however, remains the due physical proximity of ministers and faithful, so that those in the last pews can not only see and hear, but can still experience the personal relationship of belonging, and of having a meaningful function in the common action. This would unquestionably rule out the long rectangle, the one shape of a church that has been most customary, and which therefore has inspired, more than any other factor, the main objection to contemporary church planning. "It doesn't look like a church." (One wonders, in passing, whether the 4th-century Christian, worshiping in a basilica-structure adapted from a market-hall, was bothered by the same thought?) And if, to further promote better sight, the floor gently slopes toward the sanctuary, and therefore will remind some critics of a theater, what harm in that? It is a drama that they are attending, but one that requires audience participation.

Another highly desirable spatial disposition for the worshiping community is a generously proportioned transition area between street and church, an atrium-like forecourt which, if covered, could serve ideally for a baptistry, and also for friendly meeting and the consequent deepening of family charity that the eucharist has sacramentally renewed. Other auxiliary spaces, above all a weekday chapel that would contain the blessed sacrament altar, a mortuary hall, a "crying-room", for mothers with small children, are matters each community must solve according to local need—or financial capabilities!

### (4) *The Ecclesia Celebrating the Paschal Mysteries Awaits the Parousia*

Commentators on the Constitution have not been slow in singling out as one of the key *altiora principia* the emphasis on the "paschal mysteries" (cf. Arts. 5, 6, 10, 47, 61, 81, 102, 104, 106, 107, 109, 110). By contrast, the concept is lacking in *Mediator Dei*. It is a striking instance of how the Constitution has synthesized the insights of recent biblical and theological scholars on the redemptive role of the resurrection, and utilized them to clarify the inner nature of liturgical action. Organically one with this paschal outlook is the Constitution's emphasis on the fact that we constitute an *ecclesia in via;* every liturgical action is a *sursum corda,* directing our hearts to the Parousia (*e.g.,* Arts. 8, 47, 104).

The ancient Church inculcated this eschatological thinking by the orientation of its worship building, or of its ministers (and members) at prayer, and by the choice of theme for its apsidal mosaic. At a minimum, modern churches, in their construction and furnishings, should at least inspire worshipers with the joy of being "sons of the resurrection". The eucharist is the memorial of Christ's "happy" passion *and* of his resurrection, as well as of his glorious ascension to prepare a place for us. Consistently, the

Constitution therefore prefers the word "celebration" to describe liturgical actions. Sharing in the liturgy constitutes of its nature a festive occasion.

The dusky ecclesiastical atmosphere of so many "traditional" churches, designed to evoke a vague feeling of religiosity in the individual, hardly serves a communal festive rite. The house of prayer is above all a place where we assist at a eucharist which is a "paschal banquet" (Art. 47; note how St. Thomas' *sacrum convivium* has been changed to *convivium paschale*). A more generous use of light and color, the banquet table festively clothed with fine linen and flooded with light from a canopy that itself bespeaks royal triumph, such things might help inspire our faithful to make "cheerful noises" when they assemble to partake of the *convivium*. Other paschal reminders, such as a sunken baptistry from which one ascends after having received life, the paschal candle given a place of honor in the baptistry after the feast of ascension, a standing posture immediately after the consecration of mass and while receiving communion, these too can contribute to make the liturgy a personal and communal experience of the paschal mysteries.

But the *ecclesia,* however much rejoicing in the "making present" (Art. 102) of the paschal mysteries of redemption, is still an *ecclesia in via,* a Church of pilgrims whose true home is in heaven. The paschal banquet is our seed of resurrection, our pledge of future glory, the daily viaticum on our journey "until he comes" (1 Cor. 11, 26). The disposition of space in a church building should therefore reflect a people on the march; and processions are eschatologically significant. There ought, therefore, as far as possible, to be a directional polarity of the body of the faithful forward to the sanctuary, to the place where our future Judge now by anticipation is already present and confronts us in the person of his ordained minister. Lack of such an axis is one of the objections to the round or octagonal church with the altar in its center. How, in such an arrangement, is there clearly head and body, and how moreover can the head "preside" over all, greet and have dialogue with all, speak to all face to face? A means, physical propinquity, is being sought apart from its essential context and more fundamental ends. For this reason the *Richtlinien* of the German bishops have expressly rejected such a spatial arrangement, and the Montreal Directive discourages it.

## II
### THE CENTRALITY OF THE EUCHARIST

Another of the *altiora principia* of the Constitution, which will doubtless have profound repercussions in the teaching of sacramental theology and in orienting spiritual outlook, but which likewise has decisive significance for church planning, is the centrality predicated of the eucharist. The train of thought might be sketched thus: *Christ* is the High Priest; his redemptive acts climax in, and are summarized by, *death and resurrection;* this is made present by the *liturgy;* the liturgy is celebrated by the priestly *People of God* under the leadership of the ordained minister; and the compendium of the liturgy is *the eucharist.* Though the term itself is not used, the entire line of argumentation reflects recent theological thought that speaks of the eucharist as the *Ur-Sakrament,* just as the document's treatment of the Church presents it too as *Ur-Sakrament,* making present to succeeding generations *the Ur-Sakrament* who is Christ. Spiritual renewal, therefore, which is always a process of rediscovering Christ, means concretely the rediscovery of the eucharist in its full dimensions.

Press reports of the second session of the Council told how some of the Fathers considered such emphasis on the eucharist too all-embracing and exclusivist. However, the Liturgy Commission of the Council in its explanation of article 10 prior to the voting on Chapter I, instead of reducing the emphasis, cited St. Thomas (*Summa Theol.* III, 79, 1 ad 1), the Catechism of the Council of Trent and the witness of liturgical texts themselves to further extol the eucharist as "the fount of life from which all graces derive". It is the "fountain of all holiness" (secret prayer of the Mass of St. Ignatius Loyola).

### (1) *The Mass Consists of the Liturgy of the Word and the Eucharistic Liturgy*

The spatial arrangement of churches influenced by the liturgical renewal has up to most recent years reflected by its altar-centeredness an almost exclusive concern for active participation in the sacrifice. Only now, especially as a result of closer synthesis with the biblical movement and a greater sensitivity to the pastoral importance of the spoken word, is church planning beginning to wrestle seriously with the organic space relationship of ambo (and sedile) to both altar and people. This trend receives substantial impetus through the Constitution. Its manner of speaking of the "table of God's Word" and "the table of the Lord's Body" (Arts. 48, 51, 56, 106) as constituting the two parts of the mass; its declaration of Christ's "presence in his Word" (Arts. 7, 33), a biblical and patristic outlook to which for centuries we had become unaccustomed; its urging a much larger role for Scripture readings not only at mass but in other liturgical rites, as well as its encouragement of Bible services (Arts. 7, 24, 35, 51, 78, 92, 121); its restoration of the homily as an integral and normal part of the eucharistic and other sacramental rites (Arts. 24, 35, 52, 78); its stress on faith and on sacraments as "signs of faith" (Arts. 9, 33, 59), and its consequent concern for fullness and genuineness of sign in the whole program of liturgical reform, including the question of language: all these coalesce to form an *altius principium* about the importance of the Word that is bound to have major impact on architectural planning.

Some architects and liturgists have already concluded to an off-center altar, with ambo given almost equal rank on the alternate side of the sanctuary. This triangular plan, with sedile at the head of the apse, does facilitate a better view of the presiding priest. Nor is it to be denied that "the eucharistic liturgy" itself can, under one aspect, be called a "liturgy of the Word"; for it is the New Testament *berakah,* praising the Father for his merciful deeds to us in Christ: it, too, is not merely theocentric, but is *didascalia,* expressing and deepening the faith of the assembly. But the two constitutive parts of the total eucharistic rite, though historically autonomous and of independent origin, now are not equal, but complementary in unequal proportion, the service of the Word subsidiary to and leading to "the table of the Lord's Body". Christ's Word already convokes the *ecclesia,* but that *ecclesia* most fully renews its unity by eating of the same bread (1 Cor. 10,17). The "living bread" of faith prepares the assembly to receive "the living bread" of Christ's flesh (John 6), just as Christ's preaching was preparatory and contributory to the new covenant established at the last supper.

The tradition of the central altar would therefore seem eminently sound. And the ambo, by its location together with due elevation and worthy proportion, should intimate the Word's high importance of service to both altar and people. It belongs, first of all, in the sanctuary; and its place, the place of honor judged from the presiding head of the assembly's sedile, would normally be on the right or "Gospel side", *i.e.,* to the left of the main altar as viewed by the congregation.

Christ's Word, moreover, is one. And through his Word, whether in Old Testament, epistle or Gospel, he calls the assembly together into one *ecclesia,* uniting them in one faith, as by his flesh and blood he will later unite them in one common charity. It is therefore to be hoped that the reformed *Ordo Missae* will direct that the Word of God be proclaimed from one and the same ambo. The tortuous medieval allegorizing designed to justify two ambos sounds, to put it mildly, unconvincing to modern ears. Due elevation, moreover, may not be such as to suggest domination. It is a "minister" who reads, and he himself while serving others subjects himself in faith to the Word he reads. The Word of faith unites not only the people, but minister and people. Because the service of God's People through the Word will in the reformed rite likely take place for the most part at the ambo, and because the reading and praying leads into the eucharistic service, the ambo might suitably occupy a place in the fore-part of the sanctuary, closer to the congregation. This would also bring it nearer to the place where communion is distributed, thus suggesting the inner relation of "the book and the cup". In smaller churches it might even be found expedient, in order not to clutter up the sanctuary, to design an ambo that could also be the station for the distribution of the other "living bread". Evi-dently, if the people are on three sides of the altar, the ambo will have to be moved back enough so that, as far as possible, the reader faces the totality of his listeners. To the extent to which such face-to-face encounter is impossible, the spatial arrange-ment is less than ideal.

Since the Constitution so insistently extols the role of Scrip-ture, and speaks of "homily" based on Scripture and the liturgy in preference to "sermon" (*e.g.,* Art. 24), the shape of the ambo would preferably be that of a dignified bookstand or lectern rather than a pulpit. The faithful entering the church should not be distracted by a multiplicity of objects in the sanctuary, but should be able to see immediately that the mass, as the source of all holiness, offers us the book and the bread: lectern and altar, and both presided over by the priest. To reinforce the long-neg-lected stress on the Word, it has been found didactically elo-quent to place the Gospel book within an open "tabernacle" in the wide base of the lectern, to be removed only for use in the actual proclamation of the Word. Another way of achieving the same end is to have the top of the lectern on which the book rests reversible, to face reader during proclamation and people at other times. Whatever plan is chosen, the arrangement of the sanctuary space should make clear that not from bread alone does man live, not even the bread of Christ's flesh, but from every Word that proceeds from the mouth of God.

### (2) *One Altar*

A reading of all seven Letters of St. Ignatius of Antioch, who is quoted in the superb article 41, would be suitable preparatory homework for architect and client. "One God, one bishop, one faith, one eucharist, one altar." The *altiora principia* of the centrality of the eucharist, and its end which is "the unity of the Mystical Body", logically require that secondary altars, where necessary, be outside the normal visual radius of the assembly. The Constitution's article 57, 2 about concelebration points to the same conclusion; and the *Appendix* states that such altars as far as possible "should be placed in special chapels rather than in the main body of the church" (n. 4). The custom of the "his" and "her" altars in honor of Mary and St. Joseph flanking the main altar either within or without the sanctuary is a case of piety overshadowing theological principles.

Scripture, traditional liturgical texts as well as canon law most frequently refer to the altar as *mensa Domini,* the table of the Lord. The Reformation of the 16th century was, to a not insignificant degree, fought about whether there should be table or altar. It was an unfair dilemma: the place on which the eucharist is celebrated is not table or altar, but the table of the Lord which is simultaneously an altar. As a sign, the entire service of the eucharist is first of all a meal, the re-presentation of the Lord's supper, but a covenant meal which is of its nature the sacrifice of Christ's Body, delivered up for us, of his blood shed for the many. In polemical reaction to the Reformers, Catholic sacramental theology has stressed the eucharist as sacrifice, followed by the communion-meal. The Constitution, while in no wise minimizing the sacrificial character of the eucharist, in a significant shift of emphasis by comparison with Trent does not entitle the pertinent chapter "Doctrine on the Most Holy Sacrifice of the Mass", but "The Most Holy Mystery of the Eucharist", and equally significantly entitles the next chapter "The *Other* Sacraments. . . ." And it speaks of the entire service of the eucharist as "the table of the Lord's Body" (Art. 48) and as the "paschal banquet" (Art. 47).

The altar, accordingly, is the "table of the Lord", but a table "which is Christ" (cf. the rite of ordination of subdeacon) who is victim, sacrifice and altar, a sacred table which is sacramental sign of the covenant, a place of sacrificial as well as meal-encounter between man and God. Hence, Pius XII's condemnation in *Mediator Dei* (*A.A.S.* 39 [1947] 545) of a eucharistic table shaped to suggest ordinary human use. But equally misleading is the customary huge and strikingly elevated "rock of sacrifice", a "high place" accessible only to the few in fear and trembling. The altar is the table of marriage-banquet, of the sacrificial meal of which Christ invites his family to participate. An elevation of one step above the elevation of the sanctuary would not only make it appear more accessible for the people's sharing in worship and meal, but would make possible also a predella space of sufficient width for a dignified incensation all around the altar while not subtracting too much from the total sanctuary space. Moreover, since the service of the Word will most probably not be at the altar in the new reformed mass rite, the altar-table, though of worthy massiveness as to mensa and supports, need not normally be more than about two meters in length. This would be adequate even for the rite of concelebration. Such reduction of size and height, both of predella and altar, would also facilitate the congregation's view of the priest at the sedile; for if the altar is elevated by one step, the sedile could be on a platform of two steps without incurring the suspicion of being a pontifical throne. The canopy or tester, containing lights directed on the altar (and perhaps of open-grille construction allowing concentration of light from a skylight above), will of course make its contribution to the proper emphasis on the liturgical dignity and centrality of the place of eucharistic worship.

The *Appendix* adds further that the altar be free-standing and clear of all non-essentials. Moreover, "the cross and the candelabra (and only as many of the latter as are required by the particular kind of service) should be on the altar, or, according to the most ancient usage of the Church, near or around the altar" (n. 3). If the priest faces the congregation, due conclusions should be drawn about removing or reducing visually obstructive objects. Altar cards, for instance, which are memory aids and not architecturally decorative features, can lie flat on the mensa. Microphones, if necessary, should be as visually inconspicuous as possible. Perhaps it would be archeologism to suggest that the cross not be retained in the reformed mass rite as an obligatory altar adjunct. Its present rubrical necessity, dating only from the 16th century, is actually an anomaly: the priest is required to look at the figure of Christ while in the name of Christ he addresses the Father. If retained, it might well regain its original function as a processional cross. The popular custom of a realistic life-size (and even larger) figure of Christ on the cross is tautological of the altar "which is Christ", one-sidedly stresses only the "memorial" of the painful passion and death and, most censurably, is liturgically misleading since, because of its visual and emotional impact, it suggests that the eucharistic action and worship has Christ as its terminus.

### (3) *Altar Facing People*

It is needless to enter here in any detail into the legitimate pros and contras of this subject. In the light of the *altiora principia* of the Constitution, the *Appendix* simply states: "The fitting place for the main altar is midway between the presbytery and the people, *i.e.,* in the middle of the assembly (ideally not mathematically computed)" (n. 3). Priests, moreover, who have become accustomed to this orientation are almost unanimous in not wishing to revert to the former "back-to-the-people" position; and the daily experience in St. Peter's basilica during the Council has obviously won over many bishops. The chief argument for the hitherto customary position, that it better represents the priest leading his people, as it were, in spiritual procession to confront the Father, overlooks the fact that his prayers of leadership, including the canon, are invariably preceded by a dialogue which favors, if it does not demand, face-to-face confrontation. The same conclusion would result from a better balance restored to the sign value of the sacrament as meal: the head of the family does not usually preside at a table with his back turned to the other participants.

Facing the people would, obviously, bring the altar much closer to them. The principle of transcendence undoubtedly suggests a reverent distance; but this could often be additionally promoted by a more generous pre-sanctuary space and, in any event, transcendence in the New Testament, though essential in the formation of spiritual outlook in worship, may not be stressed to the exclusion or even detriment of immanence: for the glad tidings is "Emmanuel" who "has tabernacled" in our midst. To paraphrase the Lord's saying: the altar is made for man, not man for the altar.

### (4) *Altar and Tabernacle*

Again the *Appendix* indicates with some probability the future decisions of the Post-Conciliar Liturgical Commission. "It should be permissible to celebrate the sacrifice of the mass on a suitable altar facing the people, even if in the middle of the altar there is a small but precious and dignified tabernacle for reserving the blessed sacrament" (n. 6). And it goes on to suggest, especially for larger churches outstanding for their age or works of art (*i.e.*, which attract many visitors) that the blessed sacrament be reserved in a special chapel, accessible to worshipers but not to roving tourists. This at least meets the embarrassment of the June 1, 1957 decree of the Sacred Congregation of Rites, which seems to have judged "worthiness" of tabernacle solely in terms of centimeters of height. But the objections against a tabernacle on any altar during the celebration of mass are still valid, and they were best summarized by Pope Pius XII in his speech to the Assisi Pastoral-Liturgical Conference in 1956.

By intrinsic theological logic the mystery of the altar and the mystery of the reserved blessed sacrament belong together. (Reservation of the sacrament, Abbot Anscar Vonier pointed out, is merely the prolongation of the time between its confection and consumption.) But exposition of the sacrament *during the mass* (and therefore also, though in less dramatically obvious fashion, tabernacle reservation on the altar during mass) involves a conflict of mysteries. Even if the priest celebrates with his back to the people, he is merely shielding them during certain parts of the mass from facing up to the anomaly. The problem does not consist primarily in obscuring the person of the celebrant facing the people: this is in practice slight, for the psychological contact established by the very fact of his facing them outweighs the obstructive impact of the tabernacle. Nor is it chiefly a matter of tabernacle preventing view of the chalice, though this is more serious because the cup is visually the most important symbol of the sacrificial meal in which the people are expected to share. More basically, there is temporary conflict of liturgical mysteries: Christ as high priest with his Mystical Body offering the perfect sacrificial worship to the Father, and Christ the terminus of the worship proferred by his Mystical Body.

Pius XII, in conformity with the current legislation, and out of concern that any change might encourage a lessening of devotion to the real presence, nevertheless insisted on tabernacle on altar. Transference of the tabernacle to a blessed sacrament chapel will however prove no more than a partial solution, for it simply means transferring the problem to a less frequent incidence and for a smaller number of people.

The *altius principium* of receiving holy communion from particles consecrated at the respective mass (Art. 55, reiterating *Mediator Dei*), moreover, makes a tabernacle on the altar less practically needful, so that reservation can to an ever-increasing degree be restored to its original purpose of containing the species for viaticum, and for the temporally later purpose of adoration *outside of mass*.

It is to be hoped, therefore, that the further statement of the *Appendix* will be more fully spelled out and made generally legitimate: that reservation, if not on an altar, be "according to local custom in some other outstanding and suitably decorated place in the church" (n.6). This would seem to call for an ambry or sacred cupboard, not too remote from the main altar (for resorting to the tabernacle will occasionally be necessary during mass even in the most observant liturgical parish), nor within normal visual range of the congregation at mass, but easily accessible and conducive to the devotion of adorers outside of mass. If within the sanctuary, *e.g.*, at the head of the apse, a curtain could be drawn in front of it during the action of the mass, and withdrawn after mass when the sacrament again would be visually associated with the altar, thus inspiring a more "sacramental" adoration at its proper time: "O saving *Victim. . . .*" Even if the blessed sacrament is reserved in a contiguous weekday chapel, the ambry solution likewise seems better than reservation on the altar.

In either case, because of the conflict of liturgical mysteries and because of the importance of maintaining the cardinally significant liturgical principle of one altar in any one space of common worship, the present legislation about the tabernacle presents an insoluble quandary which only change according to the hint in the *Appendix* can resolve. Nor is there a solution to be found in "tradition", because the so-called Corpus Christi devotion to Christ in the blessed sacrament, however great its benefits have undoubtedly proved, developed apart from and, historically, in rivalry to the essential eucharistic piety rooted in the mass action. Article 128 of the Constitution gives added reason for hope, for it empowers "territorial bodies of bishops according to the norm of Art. 22 to adapt such things (*e.g.,* 'the nobility, placing and safety of the eucharistic tabernacle') to the needs and customs of their respective regions".

## (5) *Distribution of Communion*

A pastor remarked recently at a clerical gathering, only half-jokingly, "Our chief pastoral problem today is too many communions." Masses every hour on the hour in huge city churches built in a shape and with spatial arrangements deriving from centuries of infrequent reception of the sacrament with resultant "bottleneck" conditions at the communion rail despite three or four priests assisting, and thereby practically compelling a curtailment of the homily and the commencement of communion distribution immediately after consecration—these problems are grievous. Any church planning will therefore have to provide at a minimum for as long a communion rail as possible, and plenty of space in the "pre-sanctuary" area before the front pews, plus a

sufficient number of other aisles of adequate width to promote
easy circulation.

An even more effective solution, however, has been the in-
stallation in a growing number of churches of "communion stations" instead of a rail. The latter is not required by the rubrics,
and as a matter of fact has come to connote in the popular mind
a wall of separation from the sanctuary. Clear distinction there
must obviously be in an hierarchically constituted assembly between the clergy and laity zones. But to associate "separation"
with the sacrament whose primary purpose is unity is nothing
short of calamitous. Distinction can be obtained by difference of
elevation and by the contrast of arrangement of spaces, without
suggesting that access is physically barred to the altar which,
after all, is *the* table of the holy People's family meal.

Moreover, in the new discipline of communion under both species, reception for those who may thus communicate may likely
be at the altar itself. The communion stations, therefore, represent an answer to the problem that is both theologically and
pastorally sound. If situated at the front of the pre-sanctuary
area, at approximately the head of the various aisles, the communion "procession" can be more truly such, and experience has
proved that distribution is, paradoxically, both more reverent
and swift. The priest remains stationary, the communicants approach in double file and receive standing. As soon as one has
received, he turns outward and the next in line takes his place.
There is no searching for mouths and no suggestion of the irreverent speed that inevitably attaches to distribution at the rail.

The standing posture has moreover been urged for the Good
Friday adoration of the cross and for the same reasons that recommend it for communion. Moreover, the new Holy Week Ordo
allows communion to be distributed at stations in the church
when there is an extraordinarily large number of communicants.
But what was envisaged as an exceptional case in the Ordo is a
Sunday occurrence in many large city churches. To receive standing, moreover, besides manifesting more clearly that we receive
the living, risen Christ, and being the posture which will proba-

bly be prescribed for communion from the cup, is ecumenically significant because it restores a practice which the Western Church for more than a thousand years had in common with the Eastern Churches, who have retained it to our day.

The best height of these stations has been found to be about 42 inches for the people, and on the priest's side, about 31 inches. Distribution could of course be made to people in standing posture without the aid of constructed stations; but the latter localize the action more surely and remove any sense of uncertainty on the part of the recipients; besides, they contribute to structure more firmly the distinction between sanctuary and nave. The station for the central aisle could be movable, and setting it in place after the *Pater Noster* would help draw attention to the sacred meal that is soon to follow.

A final matter not to be overlooked: distribution from hosts consecrated at the respective mass normally requires tables for the altar breads at each church entrance, which in turn necessitates a wide corresponding aisle to avoid congestion. The rear aisle should, in any event, be broad for the sake also of an eventual stand for Bible reading and another for an intention book, in which the people are encouraged to inscribe their petitions to be remembered at the parish masses.

## (6) *Eucharist and Baptism*

The "centrality of the eucharist" means not merely that there are seven sacraments of which the eucharist is chief: the eucharist, as the Catechism of the Council of Trent quoted in the official explanation of article 10 declares, is the "fountain of all graces", the "source-fountain and other sacraments are, as it were, its rivulets". Hence in the church building in which the sacramental rites are performed, the spatial arrangements should not suggest that this is a place where, most importantly, the eucharist is celebrated and where, further, other sacraments are received; rather, the latter's organic and subsidiary relation to the eucharist should somehow be made manifest.

Among "the other sacraments" (cf. title of Chapter III), baptism occupies a unique kinship to the eucharist. Water and blood (baptism and eucharist) flowing from the side of Christ represented "the wondrous sacrament of the Church" (Art. 5); these two sacraments above all plunge man into "the paschal mystery" of Christ (Art. 6), and hence the greatest feast of the year, the Easter liturgy, is both a baptismal and eucharistic celebration. Between baptism and eucharist there is a very special axial relationship: "having been made sons of God by faith and baptism, Christians assemble to praise God in the midst of his Church, to take part in the sacrifice, and to eat the Lord's Supper" (Art. 10; cf. also Articles 7, 14, 55, 66, 67-71, 109).

This importance of baptism had been well-understood by the liturgical movement. A concern for the suitable place and furnishing of the baptistry resulted, stimulated further but also presented with new problems by the restored Easter Vigil rite.

Present rubrical legislation about the baptistry is slight: it may no longer be in a separate building, but must be an integral part of the church, though in a distinct place surrounded by a grille. Since baptism is the sacrament of initiation insofar as it introduces the person into the Mystical Body, and only thereby empowers him to partake of the eucharistic Body, the most suitable place for the baptistry would seem to be in connection with the entrance area of the church. This would not only be fitting for the rite of baptism but, especially if the font is given due structural and decorative prominence and is easily visible, it could be a moving religious experience for all who enter the church. It would remind them in an unmistakable way that only in virtue of their own baptism are they a royal priesthood, privileged to offer the sacrifice and eat of the Lord's meal, and that the holy water with which they bless themselves on entering is a sacramental radiation of their baptism, meant to cleanse them anew. In fact, if the font is in the center of the large covered atrium or forecourt, which would seem an ideal arrangement, the holy water stoups could for this purpose be attached to its grille or railing. If the baptistry is on either side of the narthex, it should ideally not only be visible to those entering, but by means of a glass or lattice wall also to those in church, for the sake of the Easter Vigil rite.

Other solutions have been sought by placing the baptistry in a transept-chapel or in a special space on either side of, but not within, the sanctuary. Because of the Easter Vigil ceremonies, the font should as far as possible be visually open to the assembly. But it would not be justifiable to conclude from the restored Easter Vigil that the font be in the sanctuary itself. The rubric directing that the baptismal water be blessed in the sanctuary space "in the sight of all" merely takes realistic cognizance of the fact that most baptistries today are not visually accessible to the assembled worshipers.

The new Easter Vigil, together with the increased awareness of the ecclesial nature of baptism and therefore of the desirability of its more public and better attended administration, calls for a corresponding spaciousness of the baptistry area. The renewal of the baptismal vows before confirmation asked for by the Constitution (Art. 71), which would most appropriately occur in the baptistry, argues to the same conclusion. The Constitution's *altius principium* of the sincerity of sign even gives ground for hope that in the new rite a true font of living water be permitted, and not only the more frequent blessing of baptismal water.

When one compares the Old Testament promises of the abundance of fresh life-giving waters that are to characterize messianic times with the spoonful of stagnant, oil-covered liquid which we have been embarrassingly pouring over the heads of our catechumens, one is led to wonder how seriously we have taken the theological principle that sacraments *"significando causant"*. Should a fountain of flowing water not be allowed, the font itself will fittingly be of a size and contain a sufficiency of water that will at least suggest a cleansing bath. Descending by steps into the baptistry, and on the opposite side ascending from it after the sacrament has been conferred, is likewise a sign of the paschal mystery of death and resurrection which would convey convincing signification to modern man. Genuineness and clarity of sign argue, finally, for a change in the baptismal rubrics: to proceed from narthex first of all into the church, and then only to the baptistry, is difficult to reconcile with the purpose of the sacrament as one of initiation into the worshiping assembly.

### (7) *Eucharist and Other Sacraments*

The Constitution, by its directives, besides stressing the polarity between baptism and the mass, admirably restores in sacramental signification the ecclesial nature of all the sacraments and their inner though subordinate relationship to their fountainhead, the mystery of the eucharist (Arts. 59, 71, 74, 76, 78, 109, 110). The purpose of the sacrament is not merely to sanctify men, but "to build up the Body of Christ and to give worship to God" (Art. 59).

Penance, in particular, presents a challenge to the church builder. The contemporary rediscovery of the ecclesial dimension of this sacrament and the disciplinary changes, which may as a consequence be permitted for certain occasions and groups of subjects, including perhaps a common preparation through an adapted Bible vigil, must be balanced with the legitimate demands of privacy. Present legislation about the place of conferring the sacrament is not very helpful. Canon law's rules, especially that about confessionals for women penitents having always to be "in an open and conspicuous place" (Canon 909), were probably not motivated primarily by liturgical preoccupations. The Constitution several times recalls the complementary character of penance and baptism (*e.g.,* Art. 109). Of its nature, penance is "the second baptism", restoring sinners to their optimum functioning as worshipers in the eucharistic assembly.

If the covered forecourt with baptistry is very spacious, it might well therefore contain one or several confessionals; in any case, toward the rear of the church is preferable to a location close to the sanctuary, both for symbolic as well as psychological reasons. Since the place of penance, further, is one where an ecclesially important sacrament is administered, this should be manifest spatially and visually. The confessional is not a "clothes-closet" conveniently recessed into the wall: it is a foreshadowing in sign of Christ's throne of mercy and judgment at the Parousia. The sacrament, moreover, is a personal encounter between the penitent and Christ in the person of the minister. Without sacrificing the anonymous secrecy that most moderns demand, there should be at least enough light in the priest's cubicle to enable the penitent to see the sacramental sign of the upraised hand, and perhaps in the penitent's, to permit the confessor to distinguish whether it is adult or teenager on the other side of the grille.

The weekday chapel, where feasible, lends itself well for the more familial rites of marriages and funerals. The "paschal character of Christian death" to be expressed in the rites of burial of the dead (Art. 81) is not enhanced by having a small group of mourners scattered about in a large church: this of itself can be a cruel experience.

### (8) *Eucharist and Devotions*

The September 1958 Instruction in its very first paragraph distinguished between *actiones liturgicae,* the liturgical actions officially performed in the name of Christ and the Church according to the liturgical books approved by the Holy See by persons lawfully deputed for this function, and *pia exercitia,* all other sacred services or actions, whether performed in or outside of church. The Constitution, in a quietly phrased but momentous modification of this all too neatly categorical division into official liturgy and private devotions, returns to a more traditional outlook by treating also of *sacra exercitia* (in contradistinction to the *pia exercitia* mentioned in the preceding paragraph): "devotions proper to individual Churches which have a special dignity if undertaken by mandate of the bishops according to customs or books lawfully approved" (Art. 13, 2). These might be called "diocesan or parish liturgy", because their recognition is based on the restored evaluation of the "local assembly", *i.e.,* of the diocese and parish as the Mystical Body in miniature. One of the ways in which they will undoubtedly find expression is the celebration of approved Bible services (cf. Art. 35, 4).

While it is salutary to recall that for about a thousand years the church building was solely limited to communal worship, and that for several centuries longer statues were unknown in Roman churches, the role of today's churches as places conducive to personal, private prayer is obviously irreversible, perhaps partly because modern man's home no longer corresponds to the conditions presupposed by Christ for "prayer in secret" (cf. Matt. 6,6). And that means, for the average parish church, aids to private devotion by means of sacred images. The Constitution's legislation in this matter mirrors its overall concern for genuineness of sign and truth.

Relics must be authentic (Art. 111); and not only should the number of images be moderate, but their relative positions should reflect right order, lest they occasion confusion and foster devotion of doubtful orthodoxy (Art. 125). The *Appendix* specifies further that the image of the titular saint may be present behind the main altar, but the figure of Christ should always occupy the more important place (n.12). The purpose of church space is therefore essentially liturgical; and the secondary, though important, aspect of aiding private devotion may not be sought at the expense of the primary. A dim religious atmosphere in the main eucharistic space in order to promote private prayer is one of the "traditions" that "is less suited to the reformed liturgy and must therefore be abrogated" (Art. 128). So, too, is the "tradition" of providing an altar for every shrine. The saints, as in the Litany of Saints, or in the famous mosaic frieze in S. Appolinare Nuovo in Ravenna, are to lead us forward to the Agnus Dei "who makes present the victory of his triumph and death" in the communal sacrifice (Art. 6). Mary herself is the prototype of the worshiping Church (Art. 103). And martyrs and saints are "to proclaim the paschal mystery" (Art. 104). To the extent that their very multiplicity distracts us from the latter, and until such time as we have regained a better perspective of what is essential and what secondary by a proper disposition of worship spaces, it may be "the better part" for the present to be prudently and orthodoxally iconoclastic.

## III

### CONCLUSION: EVOLUTION NOT REVOLUTION

Immediately pertinent are articles 21, 23 and 128 of the Constitution. But equally relevant is the context of the Constitution itself, namely the spirit that animated the Council Fathers who produced the document: a radical return to "the sources" of Scripture and Tradition in order to rediscover the true nature of the Church and interpret rightly its role in the world today.

In the history of church building and the arrangement of its parts, *the only constant* has been change. Church builders, therefore, who allow their planning to be determined by the question "Does this look like a church?" are indulging in archeologism. Not nostalgic recollections but the hard work of discovering the meaning of *ecclesia* as liturgical assembly, as well as the ecclesial role of the eucharist and the other sacraments, is primarily imperative in order to construct a building and arrange its spatial parts so that it will best serve this *ecclesia* in action. The wonderful fact is that we are today living in an age when these questions about the *ecclesia* are being asked and are beginning to be answered; while present legislation must be observed, church planning can and must therefore be guided also by a knowledgeable anticipation of the changes that the *altiora principia* of the Constitution will bring about, and as far as possible make provision for them.

In the history of church building and the arrangement of its parts, the single *greatest change has been a shift of emphasis from the priority of the living ecclesia to the ecclesia as an architectural monument.* The space to house the worshiping assembly became a more or less autonomous monument to glorify God; the *domus ecclesiae* of the earlier centuries, which had broken radically with the Old Testament tradition of the Temple, became a *domus Dei,* thereby reverting to a pre-Christian mentality. The latter's history proves, moreover, that the change took place to the serious detriment of the normal worship functioning of the living *ecclesia.* The building determined liturgical worship, and not worship the building.

It would seem, therefore, that the most imperative objective of church planners today must be a firm rejection of the "cathedral-image" that has dominated hitherto, and the return to the idea of a church structure that can be a true *domus Dei* only to the extent that it serves the local assembly, the true *ecclesia* in which God dwells. The communal and personal dimension, *i.e.,* the mystery of the Body of Christ realized in persons living in the world of today, must regain priority. The centers of cities throughout the world are overcrowded with churches which are monuments and museums if they are not ghost-structures artificially kept alive at great expense; but the millions of people in the exploding periphery and suburbs simply cannot be liturgically housed and served so long as we continue to think in terms of "monuments" which belie the very virtues that the Council Fathers have been urgently asking of Christianity today, and which the contemporary world, too, demands of the followers of Christ: evangelical poverty, simplicity, sincerity, modesty. The rejection of the spirit of "triumphalism" entails, in church forms and furnishings, an end to architectural rhetoric and the embracing of a humble spirit of service in truth.

The church is a *domus ecclesiae,* a properly functional *home* for the local worshiping assembly. Contemporary pastoral and liturgical planners may yet discover that the earliest *domus ecclesiae* known to archeologists, that of Dura-Europos in the Middle East dating from the first half of the 3rd century, a complex of spaces for baptism, catechesis and other pastoral needs, grouped around a large room for eucharisitc worship, has more than mere archeological import.

# SELECT BIBLIOGRAPHY

Of primary importance, obviously, are the *Constitution on the Sacred Liturgy,* and the *Appendix* of the Preparatory Liturgical Commission explanatory of Article 128 of the Constitution (cf. footnote 1, p. 69).

Among the directives for Church building issued by diocesan or inter-diocesan authorities may be mentioned:

"Church Building Directives for the Diocese of Superior, Wisconsin," in *Liturgical Arts* 26 (1957), pp. 7-9.

*Directoire d'Art Sacré pour le archdiocèse de Montréal,* (Montreal: Fides, 1963).

"Directoire d'Art Sacré pour le diocèse de Strasbourg," in *Bulletin ecclésiastique* 5(1955). Revised and published separately in 1957.

*Richtlinen für die Gestaltung des Gotteshauses aus dem Geiste der römischen Liturgie,* edited by Theodor Klauser (Münster: Aschendorffsche Verlagsbuchhandlung, 1947).

Cf. also "Conclusions de la Session du C.P.L." concerning "Le lieu de la célébration," in *La Maison-Dieu* 63(1960), pp. 234-9.

The following recent and several not so recent books and issues of periodicals will be found especially helpful:

"Bâtir et aménager les églises," in *La Maison-Dieu* 63 (1960).

Hammond, Peter *et al. Liturgy and Architecture.* London, 1960.

——— *Towards a Church Architecture.* London: The Architectural Press, 1962.

Henze, Anton. *Neue kirchliche Kunst.* Recklinghausen: Paulus Verlag, 1958.

Henze, Anton and Theodor Filthaut. *Kirchliche Kunst der Gegenwart.* Recklinghausen: Paulus Verlag, 1954.

Régamey, P. R. *Art Sacré au XXe Siècle.* Paris: Editions du Cerf, 1952.

Schwartz, Rudolf. *Vom Bau der Kirche.* Heidelberg: Verlag Lambert Schneider, 1938.

Seasoltz, Kevin. *Sacred Art and Architecture.* New York: Herder & Herder, 1963.

Weyres, Willy *et al. Handbuch für den Kirchenbau.* Munich: Verlag Georg D. W. Callwey, 1959.

Winninger, Paul. *Construire des Eglises. Les dimensions des paroisses et les contradictions de l'apostolat dans les villes.* Paris: Editions du Cerf, 1957.

# PART II

## BIBLIOGRAPHICAL
## SURVEY

# HELMUT HUCKE

Born March 12, 1929 in Kassel, Germany. He
studied at the Musikhochschule and at the University of Freiburg im Breisgau, where he earned
his doctorate with the thesis, "Untersuchungen
zum Begriff 'Antiphon' und zur Melodie der Of-
fiziumsantiphonen". He is editor of the *Neuen
Psalmenbuch,* co-editor of the review *Musik und
Altar,* assistant at the Musicological Institute of
the University of Frankfurt and head of the musical department of the German Historical Institute in Rome. He is the author of several important articles in musicology.

Helmut Hucke/*Neu Isenburg, W. Germany*

# Church Music

A superficial glance at the chapter on Church music in the Constitution on the Sacred Liturgy may make it appear that it contains little that is new apart from some specific directives. In fact, however, it not only imposes new tasks on Church music, but establishes completely new norms. "What the second Vatican Council did to the liturgy," says Joseph Gelineau in one commentary, "contains the seeds of a revolution, the bearing of which only future generations will be able to gauge." [1] Ernesto Moneta Caglio observes that the chapter on Church music is difficult to comment upon as future developments might well go much further than a superficial reading of the document today seems to indicate.[2] No council so far has treated of Church music in such a basic and extensive way,[3] and never have the principles which regulate the use of music in Christian worship been so completely and accurately formulated, in spite of the brevity of the chapter.

---

* Since the author repeatedly refers to the same bibliographical footnotes, these footnotes are to be found at the end of this article, pp. 132-3.

## The Basis

According to Gelineau, the most important declarations are contained in the preamble to the chapter on Church music (Art. 112). It applies the spirit and teaching of the whole Constitution to music. The function of music in worship is a *munus ministeriale*. Many commentators point out that, in contrast with the older designation of it as *umile ancilla* (Motu Proprio: *Tra le sollecitudini,* hereafter *MP*) and *nobilissima ancilla* (Const. Apost. *Divini Cultus*) of the liturgy, the present formulation avoids even the appearance of belittling it. At the same time this new designation brings out better the function and character of music in the liturgy, which leads to the conclusion that this music is the more sacred as it is more closely linked to the liturgical action.[4] The measure of its worth is therefore no longer the purely "musical" and aesthetic aspect, but rather the fulfillment of the *munus ministeriale* itself. This ought to forestall any misunderstanding that the Church holds any particular style sacrosanct.[3] The principle applies to both the rite and the performer of the rite: the singing of the preface is more important than the singing at the offertory when no procession takes place, and the *Sanctus* sung by the whole congregation at the liturgical celebration is more important than when it is sung only by the choir. The liturgical value of music does not depend on its aesthetic value but on the *"valeur liturgique du signe qu'elle constitue dans l'acte du chant."* [4]

The function of sacred song in worship leads to certain assumptions with regard to the type (reading, prayer, psalms, hymns) and to the performers, the form and the manner of performance. The Constitution, therefore, indirectly provides a code of Church music, which the Council could not work out in detail. The Council has only indicated the effects produced by music in the liturgy, and with these effects its value as a sacred sign is closely connected: (1) it expresses prayer more intimately; (2) it promotes the sense of unanimity—the true *una voce* is only achieved in the oneness of rhythm and sound in singing; (3) it lends greater solemnity to the ritual—the festive

character of the Christian liturgy is expressed in song. All forms
of genuine art are explicitly allowed as long as they correspond
to the *munus ministeriale*.[4] The Constitution in no way encourages musical poverty and it is desirable that the new kinds of
song, which will spring up in the wake of the liturgical reform,
will have the dignity of true art: music should not merely provide liturgical formation by means of notes.[2]

Having stated that its decisions have been taken with an eye
to the purpose of Church music, *i.e.*, the glory of God and the
sanctification of the faithful, the Council has defined the meaning and object of Church music in a way which is new in Church
history and has formulated a claim which ought to provoke and
stimulate musicians.[3]

## Music and the Solemn Liturgy

Almost all the commentators underline the fact that article
113 states that the criterion of liturgical solemnity lies in the
active participation of the faithful together with the singing and
cooperation of the "levites". This means that, for instance, a high
mass without the people singing is no longer the highest level of
liturgical solemnity; it is *nobiltà decaduta*.[5] And this "decides
the fate of Church concerts with a liturgical accompaniment at
the high altar".[6] This decision, however, also bestows higher
value on Church music which can now no longer appear as mere
show.[3] But article 113 not only refers to the high mass: it applies to all forms of eucharistic celebration and to all liturgical
actions. With regard to the term "levites" (*ministri sacri*) in article 113 Gelineau has pointed out that this term cannot be taken
in the literal sense because these *ministri sacri* are not employed
in all solemnly performed liturgical actions, while the functions
of lectors and cantors at a solemn celebration are obviously included.[4]

While article 113 refers the question of the language to be
used in the liturgy to articles 36, 54, 63 and 101, it seems to
dissociate this question from that of Church music.[3] But this does
not mean that it is not extremely important for Church music.

Up until now these matters were ruled by the principle that the solemn or sung celebration presupposed the use of Latin and that, apart from some exceptions, singing in the native tongue was only allowed when the liturgical service was read. Not only did this hinder the pastoral aspect,[4] but it also prevented the vigorous development of Church music, not least because this reduced Church music again to either mere decoration or accompaniment of the liturgy.

In spite of this, the new facilities granted for the use of the native tongue were not universally acclaimed by the musical profession. One article, published shortly before the announcement of the Constitution under the title "Bedroht das Vatikanische Konzil unsere Kirchenmusik?" [7] said that Church musicians could "fully appreciate the insertion of the epistle and gospel in the native tongue by the officiant" but that there were serious objections to the abolition of paragraph 14a of the *Instructio de Musica sacra et sacra Liturgia*, of 1958: *In Missis in cantu . . . unice lingua latina est adhibenda.* "Such a step would lead to a regrettable diminution of the Latin high mass, and unless a special, equally enforceable decision would make such a Latin high mass compulsory, at least on certain feasts, this would lead to the gradual disappearance of high mass." This would be "a threat to our traditional Church music".

It is true that one commentator observes: "The Constitution constantly stresses the Latin high mass as the highest form, the final goal, and this quite clearly." [8] But, on the other hand, it has been pointed out that high mass is not mentioned at all in the Constitution[3] and another commentator has noted that, contrary to what Church musicians liked to maintain up until now, article 113 does not consider the Latin high mass as the highest form and final goal of all other forms of celebration.[6] In any case, article 54 makes it clear that the faithful may speak or sing their respective parts of the ordinary of the mass also in Latin.

Ernst Pfiffner demands that where the people's active participation in the Latin high mass is already ensured, this form should be retained without question, but that at the same time the musical quality of the *Betsingmesse* should be heightened by means of choir, cantors and organ. He warns that the Latin high mass is far from superseded and that its usefulness and possibilities with regard to the people's active participation are far from exhausted. "Is it certain that those who could not discover liturgically correct and musically rich variations . . . will be able to find the right form for a *Betsingmesse* with those same means? Do they all realize that this requires *at least* the kind of preparation which had already been required by this function but had been neglected?" [9]

### The Wealth of Church Music

In fact, the traditional heritage of Church music is much less affected by the concession of the vernacular than by the principle laid down in article 28 of the Constitution: that at the liturgical celebration all, whether officiant or simple faithful, must, in the execution of their task, do all, and only that, which belongs to each in the nature of things and according to the liturgical rules (see also Arts. 29 and 30). And here, too, lies the problem contained in the wish expressed in article 114, that "the treasury of sacred music be preserved and fostered with great care". Ronald Bisegger has written: "However paradoxical it sounds, it is during the centuries of liturgical decadence that the masterpieces of Church music were created which so many are afraid of losing. Composers took the texts as proffered by the liturgy and created their masses, with their ordinary and their proper parts . . . It is now becoming clear that this kind of musical 'mass' is being called in question, to say the least, by new constructive thought which does not start from the musical point of view but from the point of view of liturgical laws and liturgical data, and which considers each sung part of the mass carefully and individually." [10] Gelineau points out that, from the point of view of the liturgical action, there are few pieces which do not demand a certain active participation by the people, and that the greater part of the present repertoire does not fulfill the required conditions. [4]

Another commentator, François Picard, also observes that it

will be necessary to examine the present repertoire carefully and to heed the principles laid down for the future if we wish each sung piece to do justice to its liturgical function.[11] "One of the outstanding features of the liturgical Constitution of the second Vatican Council is that it does not provide a catalogue of prohibitions but rather positive principles and indications. It is now up to Church musicians to consider these principles and to examine its own nature, its practice, its problems, its function and also its repertoire on this basis. Among other things it will have to investigate how far a mass by Mozart or Palestrina can be reconciled with the principles and directives of the Constitution. Such an investigation is entirely a matter for Church music and not for the Council." [3] The vital question for Church music is not how to preserve its heritage at all costs but how each sung piece and each kind of music can recover its proper function in the liturgy.

*The Choir*

Article 114 also emphasizes the formation of choirs, particularly in cathedral churches. According to article 29, members of a church choir fulfill a truly liturgical function. The choir is no longer the choir of levites (MP 19) and there are no reservations about the cooperation of women. It is no longer a substitute for a clerical choir, but a group of faithful who take over a specific liturgical function in the liturgical action.[3] Ernesto Moneta Caglio points out that today there is, particularly among the younger clergy, a tendency to look on the choir as something out of date. Such a tendency might do harm to both our musical heritage and the singing of the congregation.[2]

In the meantime, Pope Paul has dispelled the apprehensions contained in this tendency in his allocution of April 6, 1964.[12] The choir has an essential contribution to make to the liturgical and musical renewal.[13] It is the more necessary as the framework of the liturgical celebration has become more all-embracing, and even in the average congregation the choir is of great value.[4] On the other hand, it should not reduce the congregation to silence and concentrate on a repertoire far above the ordinary people.[5] An important function of the choir in the renewal of Church music is to restore the use of antiphonal singing which really has more meaning in the liturgy than singing by the people alone.

### Community Singing

With its explicit wish that choirs should be encouraged, the Constitution exhorts bishops and clergy to take great care that the whole community of the faithful play its proper part in the liturgical celebration. This preoccupation with the people is, in Hermann Schmidt's view, a characteristic feature of the Constitution and he observes that no chapter contains such a frequent insistence on the active participation by the people as that on Church music: the ten articles of this chapter contain no less than six references to it.[5]

Nearly all commentators agree that the active restitution of community singing is one of the principal tasks set by the Constitution, and that it demands exceptional effort. Ernst Pfiffner rightly stresses the fact that it is not only the fault of the choirs that the congregations do not take part in the singing. "It is easy to impose ten choral masses on the community by way of homework, and then to conclude that it does not work; it is easy to distribute some thousand refrains and new songs, but do people realize how much effort that requires . . . how long a congregation needs before it sings well, willingly and without hesitation?"[9] Is it not strange that the singing of the *Tantum Ergo* at Benediction is taken for granted but not that the people should take part in the *Sanctus* at the mass?[3]

This active restoration of community singing is not merely the business of Church musicians. It can only be brought about if clergy, Church musicians and choirs cooperate. Ernesto Moneta Caglio draws attention to a particular problem created by this emphasis put by the Constitution on community singing: it is difficult to produce music for popular singing which is also true art. But to think that true art is beyond the people and that it cannot go together with simplicity would be a mistake and would be underrating what people can do.[2]

*Liturgical and Musical Formation*

Everybody agrees that the liturgical formation of Church musicians, required by article 115, is most important in view of the great tasks that confront Church music today. But up until now this formation has been sadly neglected in many places. Both Church musicians and liturgists have to find the best ways that may lead to an improvement. On the other hand, the musical training of the clergy has also become far more important; one has but to think of the readings that must be sung in the vernacular.

*Plain Chant*

According to article 116, the Church considers Gregorian chant as proper to the Roman liturgy. It should therefore occupy first place in its liturgical actions. But the Constitution makes here a reservation which, on closer inspection, has far-reaching consequences: "Other things being equal." According to Gelineau there are here various points to be considered: How does a sung piece comply with its liturgical function; what are the pastoral conditions and needs (including the language); what are the musical abilities of those who must do the singing? [4] To give the community parts of the ordinary to sing which they cannot cope with means, in fact, to silence them.

François Picard draws attention to a certain aestheticism which is enthusiastic about the artistic value of plain chant and treats it in the spirit of *l'art pour l'art*. But this attitude empties these melodies of their spiritual contents.[14] On the other hand, the new choir movement has failed to restore to life the pieces between the readings; they are recited, even in the most important churches and on the most solemn liturgical occasions. Ernst Pfiffner points out that, with the readings being done in the vernacular, the singing of the gradual and the alleluia at high mass and in the *Betsingmesse* has become more important and literally more significant.[9]

Ernesto Moneta Caglio expects that in the future the ordinary of the mass will be sung more often by the people. But these pieces of the ordinary are late and often dubious productions of plain chant. True plain chant is found in the proper of the mass and there is a danger that it will become the special preserve of specialized choirs. The critical edition of the *Editio Vaticana,* mentioned in article 117, is the more urgent as our choir books invite many justified criticisms. It is to be hoped that this new edition will be brought out in cooperation with the critical edition of the *Graduale Romanum,* undertaken by the abbey of Solesmes,[15] and will take note of the new findings of research in musical notation.[2] A recently published plain chant textbook[16] shows how these findings, to which the work of Eugene Cardines and his school has contributed so much, have modified the presentation in the *Editio Vaticana,* and what new approaches they imply in practice.

In connection with the statement in the Constitution that the *Editio Typica* of the choir books will be completed, it is noted that an edition of the so-called German choral tradition has also been planned.[3] For the rest, various authors have pointed out that article 116 does not limit Gregorian chant to Latin texts,[17] although Gelineau observes that there is a close connection between plain chant melodies and Latin texts. Moreover, many melodies might well inspire pieces sung in other languages and there is, surely, room for adaptation and imitation.[4]

One of the recommendations of the Council is an edition of plain chant with simple melodies for use by smaller churches. The commentaries on the Constitution show what problems this creates. These problems do not so much concern the ordinary of the mass for which one or other simple melody can still be found in the manuscripts.[2] But there are serious difficulties connected with the proper. Ernesto Moneta Caglio indicates three solutions which, moreover, are already in practice here and there:

1. The use of a more or less ornate recitative for the gradual,

the verse of the alleluia and the tract, or perhaps of the formulas used for the *responsorium breve* by the gradual. But this would mean that for the sung pieces between the readings, art and natural simplicity would alternate. One may wonder whether the episcopal conferences would not prefer to have the sung pieces between an epistle and gospel in the vernacular also translated into the vernacular.

2. It might also be possible to remove the *melismata* from the melodies but this would be a very doubtful procedure.

3. Lastly, one might fit out the texts with melodies of simple antiphons from the Gregorian repertoire with similar texts or contents. That would be better than the current practice of reciting these pieces, but here, too, there would be great difficulties.[2]

Perhaps one ought to add a fourth possibility: a diminution in the number of melodies. There are, indeed, several typical melodies in the Gregorian graduals which appear with different texts. If it were possible to sing all the graduals of the liturgical year with only two or three melodies, then the needs of the smaller church would be largely satisfied because even simple choirs should be able to cope with a few frequently recurring melodies. According to Gelineau, the problem of simplifying the proper parts is not merely one of simplified melodies: it concerns the structure of the Gregorian procession antiphons. The gradual should recover the responsorial form which is a constitutive part of the religious reading service.[4]

*Religious Community Singing*

With regard to article 118 the commentaries show some uncertainty, not to say perplexity: religious community singing should be skillfully fostered, and this clearly means songs with non-liturgical texts. It even says that these texts may be used at the liturgical action, and this lifts earlier restrictions which limited this kind of singing to exceptional cases as at the German high mass. The Constitution, however, has changed the canonical situation which gave rise to the use of songs with a non-liturgical text in the liturgy, and therefore such emergency solutions are no longer required. What is necessary is to combine the requirements of the liturgy with those of popular expression.[4]

## Music in the Mission Countries

The way in which missionaries introduced Western music in their missions for centuries as a matter of course is hard to understand, even on reflection. The approach to a strange musical culture is difficult because on hearing it one judges any music involuntarily by the melody, tonality and habits of the music one is accustomed to; even specialists find it hard not to do so. Gelineau thinks this transference of Western music has succeeded here and there, but that the people's participation in the liturgy can only be secured when the music used in the liturgy is not alien to them.[4] The flowering of indigenous Church music everywhere is one of the most encouraging and satisfactory signs of our time. A start has also been made with tackling the problems that arise from the contact of indigenous music, its forms and styles with canon law and the Church's tradition in this regard.[18]

Indigenous music of countries outside Europe has an importance beyond the country of origin. According to Gelineau, many traditions have their own special values with regard to a contemplative spirituality (as in the Far East) or with regard to the musical expression of the communal sense (as in Africa), which other musical cultures do not possess to the same degree. Young nations can bring something new into the Church, just as in the 4th and 5th centuries the Syro-Greek culture and in the 9th and 10th centuries the Germanic nations left their mark on our own worship. For the rest, the problem referred to in article 119 of the Constitution not only concerns the new nations: in our own latitude liturgical expression cannot remain untouched by the ways in which contemporary man sings and expresses himself.[4]

## The Organ and Other Musical Instruments

Comments on article 120 of the Constitution, which deals with the pipe organ and musical instruments, display in various ways undisguised disappointment.[8] It has been pointed out that this is the only place in the Constitution where the notion of "ceremonies" still appears, that the organ has not been given any function in the framework of the principles laid down in article 112 and that it is still merely considered as an ornament without liturgical purpose. J. Joris asks whether the organ cannot at least be given a place in the Roman rite, and refers to St. Augustine's saying that "words fail him who is in a state of jubilation".[13] In the middle ages the pipe organ was the "royal instrument", and accordingly, another commentator would like to see it treated as the "musical symbol of Christ's royal dignity on earth", and he adds: "Its *raison d'être* clearly lies only in its presence and sound as a symbol with definite content."[8]

Gelineau points out that, unlike singing, the use of instruments is not a requisite of Christian worship. In the East the Church does not use the organ, and in the Latin Church its use is neither always possible nor opportune in every part of the world.[4] Electronic instruments are not mentioned by the Constitution. Church musicians have always opposed any concession in favor of the use of such instruments.[2] They obviously belong to the "other instruments". Insofar as they imitate the organ, which the Constitution treats with such respect, they can only be looked on as substitutes in an emergency. There is no general prohibition of any particular instrument, and this is important for Church music among the new nations: the bishops' conferences must decide what instruments can be used in public worship.

### The Vocation of Church Musicians

The section on Church music closes with a strong appeal to composers. Filled with the Christian spirit they should be aware that their vocation is to produce Church music and to increase its store of treasures. They need a personal, intimate and immediate experience of the liturgy, its spirit, its practice and its rules. One who is not an active and conscious member of a real celebrating and singing community can hardly feel the needs of such a community in himself.[4] The texts should accord with Catholic doctrine and be drawn mainly from Scripture and liturgical sources. Gelineau would like them to look beyond the liturgical tradition of the Latin Church to the tradition of Greek and Syrian hymns.[4] Many commentaries stress the need for collaboration of liturgists and composers in the editing and preparation of texts used for singing.

## The Situation of Church Music

A simple perusal of the commentaries on the Constitution gives an indication of the immense tasks Church music has to face. J. Joris speaks of the great confidence the Council has in the creative ability of our generation.[13] It is obvious that it cannot do all this quickly and at once; it will need time. This is the beginning of a period of hard work and of groping for new ways in the direction indicated by the Council.[2] What should be the starting-point for Church music and how well is it equipped for its task?

Hans Rudolf Basler's answer to the question "Does Church music do justice to the liturgical renewal?" is: "When one considers that there are still many reactionaries among composers and choirs . . . that classical mass compositions, accompanied by instruments, still dominate public worship in many places in Austria and South Germany . . . that the sung proper parts of the mass are still practically unknown to many church choirs while the ordinary parts are worn out, Sunday after Sunday, in musical arrangements which are often questionable from the point of view of both liturgy and style, then one may well give up and argue that Church music has landed itself in a situation of rigid stagnation." But this is only one side of the picture. Basler can point to some constructive developments and hopeful beginnings on the other side. "If there are composers who resist the new movement and find it difficult to escape from the status quo, it would be as easy as it would be unfair to accuse Church music, as such, of stagnation."[10]

Even where there exists lively community singing, one finds both stagnation and progress. At an international conference on

the study of the renewal in Church music and community singing, which met first at Cresuz, Switzerland, in September 1962,
then in Essen, Germany, in 1963, Erhard Quack reported on the
situation of vernacular singing in Germany; the full reports of
both conferences have been published together under the title
"Musique sacrée et langues modernes".[20]

In spite of the great and much admired tradition of hymnody
there are serious and various problems connected with vernacular
singing in German-speaking countries: vernacular hymns sung
at mass are practically all formed on the German *lied* with its
stanzas; the text only refers to the liturgy in rare, and those the
best, cases, while form and manner are still farther away from
it. Participation in the office by the people is limited, and the
services often give the impression of a poor imitation of the
Latin office. There is a lack of songs for a full share in the celebration of the liturgy by the community in the vernacular, and
the same often holds for the cantor and the schola or choir who
celebrate the liturgical action together with the community and
the celebrant. The author then gives a survey of the efforts made
to create new forms and of the problems that have found no solution as yet.[21]

*New Tasks*

At the second International Congress on Church music in
Bern in 1962, Johannes Wagner gave a lecture on "New Tasks
for Church Music in the Age of Pastoral, Liturgical Renewal".[22]
The "new" tasks are based on the "old", perennial tasks of Catholic Church music. Wagner enumerates three of them: (1) the
music must be adoration in spirit and truth, not *l'art pour l'art;*
(2) it must be a living tradition which is carried forward and
expanded. This is more than a mere "cultural" problem: the fullness of the spirit of Catholic worship can only be realized in the
historical succession of fully contemporary forms, yet containing
permanent values; (3) it must always cultivate plain chant which
is the liturgical heritage of the Western Church and the expression of its unity.

This is the basis of the "new" tasks. The question now is that Church music must take into account the "Church's awakening in the souls of the faithful". This demands: (1) "the restoration of the right distribution of musical functions at public worship, according to the structure of the community as given in the New Testament and the basic principles of the liturgy"; (2) it demands the restoration in practice of the primacy of the sung liturgy over the merely spoken one. While it is true that in liturgical law the sung celebration is recognized as the more solemn form, in practice, however, the spoken form has largely replaced it. Among specific points Wagner puts first the re-introduction of the cantor, both as soloist and as leader in antiphonal singing. Particularly where the community is no longer accustomed to taking part in the singing, the re-introduction of the cantor is the necessary first step toward the revival of communal singing.

The re-distribution of musical functions according to the structure of the community and the liturgy, and the primacy of the sung liturgy—both exactly what articles 28 and 113 of the Constitution ask for—demand new thinking. Such an attempt was made by Gelineau in his book *Chant et musique dans le culte chrétien*.[23] It then deals with the principles and the meaning of music in Christian worship: music is a constitutive, though not essential, part of the liturgy. This excludes what is profane or esoteric and *l'art pour l'art*. Church music must be sacred, not merely in the negative sense of excluding the profane, but in the positive sense that it is an integral part of worship.

It must be genuine art and have universal appeal, not in the sense of uniformity, but in the sense of unity in the same spirit within the manifold expressions of mankind. According to Gelineau, an important characteristic of Church music is that it must be functional art; for example, the singing of the gospel has the function of proclaiming the Word of God. This leads to specific requirements in music. It does not mean that Church music should be reduced to a simple utilitarian purpose as is the case with dance music or military marches; the function of art in public worship has a supernatural character. The kind, execution, performance and form of the sung pieces are connected with their function in public worship; style, musical expression, the use of polyphony and instruments depend on place and time. On this basis he determines the function of the sung pieces of the Roman liturgy and the various forms of Church singing at large, and then discusses what kind, form and execution suits them best. Finally, he compares the existing repertoire of Church music with the conclusions he has reached.

Gelineau's book has put the approach to a renewal in Church music on a new footing. For the first time an outline of liturgical reform has been worked out from the point of view of Church music. It is at once evident how indispensable the positive contribution of Church music is, not only for the practical realization of the liturgical renewal, but also for its foundation. This contribution cannot be confined to the composition of new pieces with an eye to participation by the people.

Ronald Bisegger describes it as follows: "Our thoughts run more or less like this: What is the function of the introit, the gloria, the Agnus Dei? How does music help us to understand the gradual, the sanctus, the communion? Who should sing these pieces? Which musical form is most appropriate? The cyclic form of the pieces used in the ordinary and proper parts of the mass can only be explained in the light of the history of music. But the liturgy of the mass demands a liturgical music which is set out functionally, so that everyone can make his full contribution to the execution of it according to a fitting distribution of the various parts." Instead of futile controversies about old and new, or Latin and vernacular "we should try out in detail what Church music can contribute from the tradition and what it has to create anew in a liturgy which is lived anew and as far as possible, thought anew." [10]

In an article entitled "Programme musical d'une pastorale liturgique",[24] Gelineau shows that, after communion, singing is the most important means by which the people can take part actively in public worship; so far pastoral workers have seen it mainly as useful for religious instruction. As the Church looks on the liturgy as "the summit toward which the activity of the Church is directed" and as "the fount from which all her power flows" (Art. 10), it must also consider the nature and function of singing in worship:

1. *The biblical recitative:* the proclamation of God's Word is a basic element of Christian worship. Where the community has to recite biblical texts, musical execution is simply indispensable.

2. *Psalmody:* this is the core of liturgical prayer. Without popular psalmody there will be no biblical and liturgical culture for the Christian people nor will they take part in liturgical singing. This does not mean that only the people sing the psalms. The traditional form is a responsorial psalmody in which cantor or choir alternates with the community. In this way it expresses that the psalm is God's Word addressed to the people; the community receives it and replies with a refrain.

3. *Acclamations, litanies and prayers:* acclamations express the community's assent to the public prayer of the celebrant and replies to it. In the litanies the community falls in with the needs as formulated by the celebrant. In the solemn prayer of the eucharist the community "acclaims" with the call of *"Sanctus";* in the canon of the Latin rite the people's acclamations have been reduced to silence.

4. *Processional songs:* in the mass particularly the introit, offertory and communion, and also the alleluia can be considered as the processional song for the gospel. The rule is that a procession is accompanied by a song which reveals its spiritual meaning and which turns it into a communal action. Comparison with other rites shows that processional songs are not psalmody in the strict sense, but link a particular text (the antiphon) with verses from the psalms.

### The Sung Proclamation in the Vernacular

After the announcement of the Constitution, Church musicians became sharply aware of the problem of melodies to be used for the readings in the vernacular. In an article entitled "Le récitatif liturgique en langues modernes", I have suggested that the recitative is as much a basic form of singing as the *Lied* or the *Jubilus,* with a very definite function and a vital place;[26] the sung proclamation cannot replace the recitative by some other form of music. The article then investigates the principles and laws of the recitative and its components and so tries to discover the basic requirements for a liturgical recitative in the vernacular. The greatest problem lies in its rhythm: the training for careful, appropriate and noble speaking in free rhythm is decisive and perhaps more important than the recitative tune itself.

According to Urbanus Bomm's article, "Zur Vortragsweise liturgischer Lesungen in deutscher Sprache",[26] the sung execution of readings in modern languages is to be rejected: for Israel and the first Christians the sung reading corresponded to their image of God and man. For contemporary man "God no longer sings", and the spoken delivery is "the more genuine expression of the Word's appearance among the people of our own language." The problem is more thoroughly dealt with from various aspects in one number of the periodical *Eglise qui chante.*[27] Answering the question "Faut-il chanter les lectures en français?" Gelineau maintains that in the solemn liturgy the sung reading is traditional and that it is hardly tolerable that in a celebration in which singing is a most important element, precisely this element would fall out at the proclamation of God's Word. Yet, there are real problems:

1. In contemporary French culture the arts of speech and music have become autonomous. Rhetorical speech is no longer sung but spoken.

2. In the past the sung delivery helped understanding. Today we have loudspeakers. Good loudspeakers bring a vitality of tone which escapes the impersonal sung delivery.

3. A well-sung reading of the gospel may be a grand experience, but the sung gospel of a Sunday after Pentecost may sound pretentious to a community that follows the text in the missal. One may nevertheless hope that there will be a gradual psychological change that will bring about greater solemnity in ordinary celebrations.

4. All readings of the liturgy are sung without reference to their specific literary form. Today we have become more sensitive on this point. Certain parts of Scripture (*e.g.*, the prologue of St. John, the story of the creation, the passion according to Matthew and John) lend themselves excellently to singing. Other readings, which contain a series of exhortations addressed to the community, seem to jar with singing.

5. In seminaries the Latin singing of readings is taught according to definite formulas. Our theologians have not been prepared for the sung recitative in the vernacular. But this holds also for the spoken delivery: the training of seminarians for song and speech is of one piece; it will be most important for the liturgical renewal.

Gelineau concludes that sung readings are good and desirable in certain cases but that they are not possible, without further qualification, in all sung masses for all congregations and with all types of texts. In another contribution he discusses the singing of readings in French. In "De la cantillation, sa nature et les conditions de sa réalisation", Jean-Yves Hameline treats the problem phenomenologically: singing puts the Word outside everyday experience, it does not stir the emotions, is not individual, has a ritual character and suggests the timelessness of the mystery. The Christian people is incapable of seizing this transcendency, it personalizes God. On special occasions, however, a celebration rises above the everyday level. So, starting from a different angle, Hameline reaches the same conclusion as Gelineau. He also points out that it is not enough for a cantor to master the delivery technically when he sings the readings. It is not a matter of having a fine voice; he must be aware of what he proclaims and this must come out in his delivery.

In "Récitatifs pour la proclamation solennelle de la parole de Dieu", Lucien Deiss gives some practical hints. Finally, there is an exchange of opinion and some guidance on "Comme je prépare le récitatif d'une lecture". Josef Schabasser contributes some indications on how to use the Latin *tonus communis* for a reading in German.[28] The difficulties that beset the sung readings in

the West will not be the same for all other cultures, and even in
the West these problems are not everywhere identical. But the
example of the liturgical recitative shows precisely how useful
and important it is to exchange experiences on an international
level where liturgical singing in the vernacular is concerned.

*Psalmody—Processional Songs—Hymns*

Starting from the widespread success and effectiveness of Gelineau's psalmody, Ernesto Moneta Caglio has contributed a critical examination[29] and offers various suggestions and objections:
the preoccupation with community singing should not sacrifice
the role of the choir. The literal translations of the psalms show
up the problems of Semitic forms and suitability for singing, a
point that also crops up in the *Psalterium Pianum*. Liturgists are
often uncritical where music is concerned, while musicians are
often too critical about popular singing. Gelineau's work is important and has great merit. But one should remember that it is
still only a beginning, a first attempt. One cannot overlook other
forms apart from psalmody. On the other hand, one cannot limit
oneself to imitating the example set by the French.

Gelineau's article, "Les Chants processionaux. Recherches sur
leur structure liturgique",[30] shows that the real structure of the
processional songs has been overlaid by the developments in plain
chant and has become unrecognizable. Comparison with Eastern
rites shows the following: processional songs link biblical or
non-biblical refrains with verses from the psalms. The verses from
the psalms are sung by soloists, the refrains by the choir, while
the people participate by joining in at the end of the refrain or by
singing a *versus ad repetendum*. This form of processional song
suits the procession particularly well and it would be worthwhile
to restore this traditional form. Gelineau adduces some examples
of how the introit can again be shaped as a processional song.

Bernard Huijbers reports on a remarkable attempt in the field
of hymnody.[31] In cooperation with Huub Oosterhuis,[32] he has
created songs which are to be sung after the gospel or the homily
and which, by making the people use sentences from the gospel,

allow them to respond to the message of the gospel. These songs mostly have refrains and show, once again, the importance of alternate singing for the renewal of Church music. They are at the same time an excellent contribution to the rebirth of song in the Church in the sense of a communal song in the musical language of our own days. With his attempt, which grew out of awareness of pastoral needs, Huijbers unintentionally created a link with the old forms of singing in Christian worship that were lost in the Roman rite.

# BIBLIOGRAPHICAL FOOTNOTES

[1] Joseph Gelineau, "Die Reform der Liturgie. Zur Bedeutung der Konzilskonstitution vom 4th. 12.1963," in *Wort und Wahrheit* 19 (1964), pp. 169-83.

[2] Ernesto Moneta Caglio, "Il Concilio Vaticano e la Musica sacra," in *Musica sacra* (Milan) 88, 2nd ser. 9 (1964), pp. 36-48.

[3] Helmut Hucke, "Die Kirchenmusik in der Liturgiekonstitution des 2. Vatikanischen Konzils," in *Musik und Altar* 16 (1964), pp. 8-16.

[4] Joseph Gelineau, "Deuxième Concile du Vatican. La Constitution sur la liturgie. Commentaire complet. Ch. VI: La Musique sacrée," in *La Maison Dieu* 77 (1964), pp. 193-210.

[5] Ermanno Schmidt, "Il popolo cristiano al centro del rinnovamento liturgico," in *La Civiltà cattolica* 115 (1964), pp. 120-31.

[6] Norbert Höslinger, "Die neue Konstitution über die heilige Liturgie. Ein Kommentar II," in *Bibel und Liturgie* 37 (1963/64), pp. 248-49.

[7] Franz Kosch, "Bedroht das Vatikanische Konzil unsere traditionelle Kirchenmusik?" in *Singende Kirche* 11 (1963/64), pp. 53-57.

[8] Clemens Reuter, "Chor und Orgel—noch zeitgemäsz?" in *Im Dienste der Kirche* 45 (1964), p. 160.

[9] Ernst Pfiffner, "Streiflichter zur Liturgiereform," in *Katholische Kirchenmusik* 89 (1964), pp. 128-36.

[10] Ronald Bisegger, "Bausteine für eine neue Liturgie," in *Katholische Kirchenmusik* 89 (1964), pp. 125-28.

[11] François Picard, "Commentaire" (on the Constitution), in *Musique et Liturgie* 97 (Jan.-March 1964), pp. 2-4.

[12] Paul VI, "Message lors du pèlerinage des Chorales liturgiques à Rome, le 6 Avril 1964," in *Jubilate Deo* 11 (Ascension 1964), pp. 1-3.

[13] J. Joris, "De Kerkmuziek na de Constitutie over de Liturgie," in *Musica sacra* (Malines), 65 (1964), pp. 75-94.

[14] François Picard, "A temps nouveaux musique nouvelle," in *Musique et Liturgie*, 96 (Nov./Dec. 1963), pp. 1-4.

[15] "Le Graduel romain. Edition critique par les Moines de Solesmes." So far have appeared: Vol. 4, Le Texte neumatique. Vol. 1, Le groupement des manuscrits. Vol. 2, Les relations généalogiques des manuscrits (Abbey of S. Pierre de Solesmes, 1960 and 1962).

[16] Luigi Agustoni, *Der Gregorianische Gesang* (Freiburg Br., 1963).

[17] *Liturgisches Jahrbuch* 14 (1964), p. 93, and Ferdinand Kolbe, "Die Liturgiekonstitution des Konzils, II: Praktische Hinweise," in *Liturgisches Jahrbuch* 14 (1964), p. 134.

[18] Stephen B. G. Mbunga, "Church Law and Bantu Music. Ecclesiastical Documents and Law on Sacred Music applied to Bantu Music," in *Neue Zeitschrift für Missionswissenschaft*, Suppl. XIII (Schöneck-Beckenried, Switzerland, 1963).

[19] Hans Rudolf Basler, "Wurde die Kirchenmusik der liturgischen Erneuerung gerecht?" in *Katholische Kirchenmusik* 89 (1964), pp. 118-20.

[20] *Musique sacrée et langues modernes. Deux colloques internationaux* (Kinnor, Vol. 4, Paris 1964).

[21] Erhard Quack, "Facture musicale et Chants d'Assemblée," in *Musique sacrée et langues modernes,* pp. 39-52. In German: "Musikalische Gegenwartsprobleme des liturgischen volkssprachlichen Gesanges," in *Musik und Altar* 15 (1963), pp. 80-85.

[22] Johannes Wagner, "Neue Aufgaben der katholischen Kirchenmusik im Zeitalter des pastoralliturgischen Erneuerung," in *Liturgisches Jahrbuch* 13 (1963), pp. 22-29.

[23] J. Gelineau, *Chant et musique dans le culte chrétien* (Kinnor, Vol. 1, Paris 1962).

[24] J. Gelineau, "Programme musical d'une pastorale liturgique," in *Musique sacrée et langues modernes,* pp. 17-38.

[25] Helmut Hucke, "Le récitatif en langues modernes," in *Musique sacrée et langues modernes,* pp. 59-78. In German: "Erwägungen über das Rezitativ und das Problem liturgischen Rezitativs in der Muttersprache," in *Musik und Altar* 16 (1964), pp. 49-59.

[26] Urbanus Bomm, "Zur Vortragsweise liturgischer Lesungen in deutscher Sprache," in *Musica sacra* (Cologne) 84 (1964), pp. 202-10.

[27] "Le Chant des Lectures," in *Eglise qui chante,* 55/6 (1964).

[28] Josef Schabasser, "Der Gesang des Evangeliums in deutscher Sprache," in *Singende Kirche* 11 (1964), pp. 192-94.

[29] Ernesto Moneta Caglio, "Il canto popolare religioso e P. J. Gelineau," in *La Rivista del clero italiano* 45 (1964), pp. 23-36.

[30] J. Gelineau, "Les chants processionaux. Recherches sur leur structure liturgique," in *Musique sacrée et langues modernes,* pp. 105-18. In German: "Art und Form der liturgischen Prozessionsgesänge," in *Musik und Altar* 16 (1964), pp. 16-19 (abridged).

[31] Bernard Huijbers, "Nouvelles hymnes sur les Evangiles," in *Musique sacrée et langues modernes,* pp. 77-95. In German: "Evangelienlieder. Ein neuer Versuch," in *Musik und Altar* 16 (1964), pp. 60-8.

[32] Huub Oosterhuis, "Verantwoording van een liturgisch Experiment," in *Tijdschrift voor liturgie* 46 (1962).

# HENDRIK MANDERS, C.SS.R.

Born February 2, 1913 in Roosendaal, Netherlands. He became a Redemptorist and was ordained September 22, 1939. He pursued further studies at the Angelicum in Rome and the Pontifical Oriental Institute where he earned his doctorate with the thesis, "De liefde in de spiritualiteit van S. Alfonsus". He is professor of dogmatic theology and of liturgy at the Redemptorist seminary in Wittem, Netherlands. He has published several articles and has contributed to the *Theologisch en Liturgisch Woordenboek*.

Hendrik Manders, C.SS.R. / *Wittem, Netherlands*

# Concelebration

*Concelebratio liturgica fecundioribus et gloriosiori-*
*bus S. Matris Ecclesiae Catholicae traditionibus ac-*
*censenda est.*                    Dom Pl. De Meester

Today's interest in concelebration may appear new, but it is not quite as recent as it may seem at first sight. A look at past literature[1] and a careful analysis of it show that in the Western Church there has been for some fifty years a movement leading to the situation that the recent decisions of Vatican Council II have taken as a new starting-point.[2] This

---

[1] For an extensive bibliographical survey see H. Schmidt, *Introductio in liturgiam occidentalem* (Rome, 1960), pp. 406-10. For the years 1898-1958 there are 59 items. The list was brought up to 1963 (a total of 75 items) by the author in a stencilled bibliography which was distributed to those who took part in the days of study at Trier in 1963. Later contributions are mentioned in the studies by Danneels and Tihon, referred to in note 28. The perusal of Schmidt's list alone shows a number of interesting topics. It is easy to see, for instance, where there was interest in concelebration before Vatican Council II brought it out. Of these studies, 33 are in French, 10 in German, 9 in Dutch, 8 in Spanish, 5 in Latin, 4 in Italian (of the 42 French and Dutch ones, about 20 are written by Belgian authors). Several Italian and German studies do not deal directly with concelebration but with related issues, such as the "fruits" of the mass, frequency of celebration, etc.

[2] *Constitution on the Sacred Liturgy,* articles 57 and 58.

movement has had its ups and downs.[3] It is, therefore, the more interesting to see how in Vatican Council II, and the literature connected with it, the original inspiration emerges on a new level.

It is proposed here to present the results of some five more recent studies. Before that, it is perhaps useful to show which influences led to this new interest in concelebration in the West.

## I

### THE GROWTH OF AN ATTITUDE

As has been said, interest in concelebration is already old in the Western Church. There are, however, two kinds of interest. The first covers the period from the medieval theologians to the origin of the liturgical movement, more or less. During this time it was a rather incidental interest and mainly concerned with a somewhat recent form of concelebration, namely, that taking place at the ordination of a priest or the consecration of a bishop. This interest was not very favorable to concelebration. The most that could be said in favor of it seems to be St. Thomas's phrase *nihil refert*.[4] It contained no encouragement and it may well be

[3] Not only is there a gap in the literature between 1932 and 1949, but in official circles there appears some opposition to the postwar desire for concelebration. The reason for this seems to lie in the fear of depreciation of the private mass which was such an important element in a priest's spirituality and which supporters of the *messe communautaire* and concelebration opposed in a not always very elegant manner. We cannot deal with this question here, but refer to the statement of the French episcopal commission about this and related controversies: "Note de la commission épiscopale de pastorale et de liturgie," in *LMD* 34 (1953), pp. 145-56 (with a commentary by A. M. Roguet, which prompted a reply by the commission in *LMD* 36 [1953], 8). Cf. *EL* 67 (1953), pp. 347-49; *QLP* 34 (1953), pp. 179-82; *Doc. Cath.* 50 (1953), pp. 585-87. In that same year, 1953, Fr. J. Löw wrote to me: "Rome, today, and especially the Congregation of Rites, which has competence in the matter, is strongly *against* any attempt to introduce concelebration" (letter of August 9, 1953; italics by Löw). The situation has since changed basically as a result of penetrating investigations on both sides.

[4] *Summa Theol.*, III, q. 82, a. 2 ad 2: *Sed quia sacerdos non consecrat nisi in persona Christi, multi autem sunt unum in Christo, ideo non refert utrum per unum vel per multos hoc sacramentum consecretur.* . . . For a recent survey of scholastic opinions, see M. Nicolau, "La concelebración eucaristica," in *Salmanticenses* 3 (1961), pp. 269-94; *id.*, "Problemas del concilio vaticano II," in *Vision teologica* (Madrid, 1962), pp. 139-72.

that the strict line taken by the Codex[5] is due to that perspective. The reason is that the theologians were not interested in the meaning of concelebration but rather in the validity of the consecration; moreover, they lived in a spiritual climate where concelebration could not really be understood.[6]

In the nineteen-twenties there was, however, a change in the atmosphere, limited at first to a small circle of professional theologians. But these theologians spoke out and broadcast their ideas. They threw the stone in the water and the circle of its influence expanded until it covered the situation on which the Council has now legislated.

One may say that two factors have contributed to this change. The first developed in Rome and is permanently linked with the name of Pius XI: a more profound contact with the life of the Eastern Churches which deepened liturgical and theological thought here. In 1923 Dom Placidus De Meester addressed cardinals, bishops and other dignitaries in connection with a concelebration that took place in the *Chiesa nuova*. He had to warn his audience discreetly that concelebration was "a liturgical function . . . perhaps unknown to many".[7] In this address he

---

[5] Can. 803: *non licet pluribus sacerdotibus concelebrare, praeterquam in missa ordinationis presbyterorum et in missa consecrationis episcoporum secundum pontificale romanum.* The canon clearly assumes concelebration.

[6] I cannot omit to quote here what Dom Beauduin had already written in 1922: "Two questions might arise. Can priests of the second class offer the sacrifice *separately?* Would not the unity of the Church be compromised in its most efficacious and sacred function, if a priest apart from his bishop could celebrate the mysteries outside of the important hierarchic context that we have described? In other words, is not concelebration obligatory? . . . But later . . . the question arises on the opposite side. Seeing that priests of the second class are endowed, just as their bishops are, with the power of offering the body and blood of the Savior, would it really be proper for them to offer the sacrifice on their part only by being united to their hierarchic superior? In other words, is concelebration really *licit?*" L. Beauduin, "Concélébration eucharistique," in *QLP* 7 (1922), pp. 276-7.

[7] Pl. De Meester, "De concelebratione in Ecclesia Orientali, praesertim secundum ritum byzantinum," in *EL* 37 (1923), pp. 101-10, 145-54, 196-201. The quotation is on p. 102 and has also provided the motto of this article.

defended the basic principle—somewhat obscured in the nineteen-fifties, as will be seen—that the meaning of concelebration is "to express, first, the communal character of the Church's prayer; secondly, the principle of the hierarchic nature of the Church and, thirdly, the close bond of unity which the Church received from her Founder".[8]

The second factor appeared at about the same time. It was the liturgical movement that became aware of its pastoral function. Dom Beauduin, who also had close ties with the East, wrote his article in *Questions Liturgiques et Paroissiales*.[9] He, too, emphasized the Church's hierarchical unity as the meaning of concelebration.[10] At the Eucharistic Congress of Amsterdam he put these thoughts before a wider public.[11]

Finally, at the end of the nineteen-twenties and the beginning

---

[8] *Art. cit.*, p. 198: "Concelebratio siquidem apte exprimit sive *characterem socialem* ecclesiasticae precis, sive principium hierar-*chicum* essentialiter Ecclesiae inhaerens, sive tandem *unitatem* arctissimam qua Ecclesia a suo divino Auctore instructa fuit" (italics of the author).

[9] L. Beauduin, "Concélébration eucharistique," in *QLP* 7 (1922), pp. 275-85 and 8 (1923), pp. 23-4. A. Paladini, who summarized this in *EL* 37 (1922), pp. 400-5, 422-24, agrees with Beauduin's wish for a restoration of the practice and adds the following striking quotation: ". . . The reader will wonder whether there is any chance that these ancient rites might be restored in modern liturgical law. We do not think so. In any case it will not take place in our generation. But this great Christian principle of hierarchic unity within the Mystical Body, of which these ceremonies were the public and solemn profession, must surely be restored sooner or later. . . . The eucharistic mysteries are the divine institution that is the most fruitful source and the most expressive symbol of this unity. There is no need of a catechism formula or a pastoral letter to teach this principle. By slow infiltration and, as it were, by osmosis, the liturgy . . . especially if it recovers one day its traditional fullness . . . can contribute to the remaking both of individual Christians and of a true Christianity" (*QLP* 8, 1923, p. 34).

[10] ". . . la notion profonde qui a inspiré le rite concélébratoire c'est l'unité hiérarchique de l'Eglise . . ." (*art. cit.*, *QLP* 7, 1922, p. 277).

[11] L. Beauduin, "La concélébration eucharistique" in *Congrès eucharistique d'Amsterdam 1924*. In his article "La concélébration," in *LMD* 7 of 1946 (pp. 8-26) he stresses his points once again, confronting his position with the "crisis" of the private mass, and, as his hopes of realization have increased, he puts forth some suggestions in connection with a possible restoration. Note his three conditions: only with the local bishop presiding; reserved for great and solemn occasions; with special rubrics to be laid down by Rome (*art. cit.*, pp. 22-3).

of the nineteen-thirties, there appeared an historical study, again from someone closely connected with the East.[12] It was a truly basic study that exercised great influence on the discussion during the following twenty years. Not only did the author gather and interpret the historical evidence on which most later studies were based, but he also introduced the distinction between sacramental and ceremonial concelebration. This distinction, peculiarly misunderstood, was going to play an important part in postwar discussion and lead to a formulation of the problem which was not intended by the writer and which contributed considerably to a false perspective.[13] The author of this article, J. M. Hanssens,[14] is a third Belgian—a Jesuit after two Benedictines—connected with the papal Oriental Institute.

After Hanssens' work the field lay quiet, but it did not lie fallow. Apparently the theologians did not take notice.[15] The first

---

[12] Because of limited space this article does not deal with problems concerning the history of concelebration. Not everyone follows Hanssens' interpretation. Cf. B. Botte, "Note historique sur la concélébration dans l'Eglise ancienne," in *LMD* 35 (1953), pp. 9-23, and N. Afanazieff, *Trapeza Gospodjna* (Paris, 1952). A summary of the latter work may be found in B. Schulte's review of it in *CCP* 19 (1953), pp. 441, 443-49.

[13] Hanssens has stressed that his distinction is purely descriptive: in the *concelebratio sacramentalis* the words of consecration are *de facto* pronounced by all simultaneously; in the *concelebratio caeremonialis* this is not the case. He does not deal with the theological problem: which of the two is "co-consecratory" (cf. *Periodica* 16 (1927), pp. 143-44; 21 (1932), p. 219). In his later studies his opinion seems to harden. Cf. J. M. Hanssens, "La concelebrazione sacrificale della messa," in *Eucaristia* (Rome 1957), pp. 809-26, and "La concelebrazione sacrificale della messa," in *Divinitas* 2 (1958), pp. 240-66.

[14] J. M. Hanssens, "De concelebratione eucharistica," in *Periodica* 16 (1927), pp. 143-54, 181-210; 17 (1928), pp. 93-127; 21 (1932), pp. 193-219.

[15] No textbook known to me deals with the question. Even the extensive bibliographies in M. Schmaus, *Katholische Dogmatik* III, 13-5 (Munich 1958), do not mention any studies on concelebration. Hanssens' name does not even appear. The first edition of *LThK* has no reference to "Konzelebration" (Jungmann and Rahner have dealt with it in the second: *LThK* 6, 2nd ed., pp. 524-5). Concelebration was obviously considered to be a liturgical problem, not a theological or sacramental one. The need for a dogmatic approach begins to be felt in the nineteen-fifties. A few theologians "risk" it; cf. K. Rahner, "Dogmatische Bemerkungen über die Frage der Konzelebration," in *Münch. Theol. Zeits.* 6 (1955), n. 2; *id.*, "Dogmatique de la concélébration," in *QLP* 36 (1955), pp. 119-35;

German reaction appeared during the war,[16] in Spain, and not until 1949 in Holland.[17] But by then a new factor had appeared on the scene.

This factor might be described as a change in the Western attitude toward the celebration of mass. It was a factor that was found to stimulate a general leavening process because it was not yet mature itself. It carried traces of old-fashioned Western issues and attitudes toward the mass. It brought out particularly the newly reviving social aspect of the mass without, however, doing full justice to its specific communal character (which Hanssens so deeply impressed on his disciples). It introduced an opposition to the existing but antiquated individualistic forms of celebration and thereby provoked resistance from other groups and from the authorities. The hierarchy made decisions which seemed to delay the development of concelebration but which helped the issue by stimulating theological research. All this brought concelebration to the phase in which it is now recognized by the Council.

The appearance of this factor was partially due to a very practical problem that arose after the war. This period, indeed, brought the phenomenon of relatively large conferences of priests (with or without the laity), and this showed up the inconvenience of a multitude of private masses. Those who have experienced the horror of this truly unfitting type of celebration do not need any further explanation, and those who have not will consider themselves fortunate when they read about the complaints made by various authors. In any case, a remedy had to be found, and since concelebration was canonically impossible, another solution was suggested, a *messe communautaire* of the clergy. This consists in one priest celebrating in the strict sense while the other priests

---

G. Frenaud, "Remarques doctrinales au sujet de la concélébration," in *QLP* 37 (1956), pp. 114-28.

[16] H. v. Meurers, "Die eucharistische Konzelebration," in *Pastor Bonus* (Trier) 53 (1942), pp. 65-77, 97-105.

[17] D. Alarcia, "La concelebración," in *Liturgia* (Silos) 4 (1949), pp. 124-26—only a brief article, as is clear. J. Delièvre, "Concelebratie," in *TL* 33 (1949), pp. 11-27. The author concludes: "I doubt whether it is desirable at present to restore the practice of concelebration publicly in

participate. We do not wish to write at length about the problems created by this *messe communautaire,* but it has to be mentioned because it led to new problems connected with concelebration. It soon became evident, indeed, that this type of celebration implied a tendency toward concelebration in one way or another[18] and thus put concelebration in a new light, but also in fresh difficulties.

The first question that arose concerned the relation of the *messe communautaire* (and by implication, of concelebration) to the private mass. This point gave rise to a number of theologically unpalatable or abstruse questions. There were abstruse questions about the greater or lesser value of a large number of private masses as compared with one mass collectively celebrated by many priests.[19] Here Pius XII, influenced by Hürth, a theologian of the Holy Office, took up a position in two addresses that still puts great obstacles in the way of theological penetration.[20]

Behind this, however, lay a much more searching question that is important for the spirituality of the priest: how much is individual celebration a positive element in self-sanctification and the

---

our cathedrals and churches, *e.g.,* on the great feasts of the liturgical year, because in their present mentality the ordinary faithful, accustomed to assess the degree of solemnity of a mass by the number of participating priests, will either not or with great difficulty understand the distinction between concelebrating priests and assistant priests" (p. 27).

[18] This is clearly shown in the article by J. Tillard, "Concélébration et messe de communauté," in *QLP* 43 (1962), pp. 22-35.

[19] This very controversial question, too, cannot be dealt with here. Cf. K. Rahner, *Die vielen Messen und das eine Opfer* (Freiburg, 1951), of which a preliminary study appeared in *ZKTh* 71 (1949), pp. 257-317; *id.,* "Die vielen Messen als die vielen Opfer Christi," in *ZKTh* 77 (1955), pp. 94-101. For the controversy in France, see note 3, and also, A. Michel, "Questions posées: célébration privée et communion à une messe communautaire," in *AmCl* 63 (1953), pp. 440-43; G. Frenaud, "Concélébration et messes communautaires," in *Facultés catholiques de l'ouest;* Bull. trim. n. 2 (April, 1954), pp. 43-58; n. 3 (July, 1954), pp. 29-38. See also G. Liesting, "Het veelvuldig mislezen," in *SSma Eucharistia* 47 (1955), pp. 71-7; "De zin en het goed recht van de vele missen," *ibid.,* pp. 135-40; "De algemene vrucht van het misoffer en het goed recht van de privaatmis," *ibid.,* pp. 165-70; "Concelebratie," *ibid.,* pp. 257-62, 289-95.

[20] Allocution of Nov. 2, 1954, in *AAS* 46 (1954), pp. 668-70; allocution of Sept. 22, 1956 (after the Congress of Assisi) in *AAS* 48 (1956), pp. 716-18. The text also appears in H. Schmidt, *Introductio,* pp. 401-5.

spiritual life of the priest? And this leads to the question of the frequency of celebration: is daily celebration a genuine spiritual value? [21] In the discussion on concelebration these questions strongly emphasized an element that was little stressed in the previous studies concerned with the *meaning* of concelebration, though it was brought in as part of the discussion on the interpretation of the historical evidence,[22] namely, as the desire to allow all participating priests to renew Christ's sacrificial act individually by pronouncing collectively the words of consecration. The question of concelebration (or communal celebration) became a question of co-celebration (or collective celebration). A situation threatened in which concelebration would become a practical solution only where many priests could not celebrate both individually and simultaneously, and where, as one author observes, the celebration becomes a synchronized mass in disguise.[23]

Another element, however, combined with this. Precisely because the *messe communautaire* of priests was experienced as a communal action that showed the solidarity of the *priests* among themselves, and made the contrast felt between this and the individual private mass in an isolated corner, and because concelebration was seen as the ideal expression of this communal bond,

[21] Apart from the authors referred to in note 19, see also Th. Vismans, "Concelebratie," in *TL* 42 (1958), pp. 297-305 and 44 (1960), pp. 329-43. Particularly in the second article the author deals extensively with the question of how correct the present norm is for the frequent celebration of mass (*l.c.*, pp. 329-36). Cf. *Lit. Wdb.*, col. 449f.

[22] An important part was played here by the question whether the silent concelebration, which was doubtless the original one and is still in use outside the Byzantine-Slavonic and Uniate rites, was "co-consecratory", but there is no room to deal with this here.

[23] B. Botte writes: "Concelebration would appear to be the way of reconciling the multiplicity of masses with a ceremony that would be more expressive of the communal character of the mass and of the unity of the Church. Thus concelebration is conceived as the synchronization of many masses" ("Note historique sur la concélébration dans l'Eglise ancienne," in *LMD* 35 (1953), p. 9.) This is also the reason why several important authors treat the spoken concelebration with a certain hesitation. It was already put forward by J. M. Hanssens in "De concelebratione eucharistica," in *Periodica* 21 (1932), p. 217: *Dubium non est quin ista unitas in caeremoniali quam in sacramentali concelebratione manifestius appareat, cum illa ritus praecipui unitatem perfecte servat et etiam in eo singularem partem principali celebranti tribuat, haec vero in secundaria*

as the point toward which the *messe communautaire* tended—precisely because of all this, concelebration was too easily thought of as the celebration of the unity of the priesthood itself.[24] No longer was it thought of primarily as total celebration with the people, but only insofar as priests belong together. Thus, in the middle of a period in which the liturgy was going to be de-clericalized, there arose a tendency toward clericalization of concelebration. This clericalization was encouraged by the above-mentioned tendency toward co-celebration.[25]

The principle of concelebration as manifestation of the hierarchical unity of the Church, so strongly emphasized by the older authors in conformity with tradition, found itself in competition with the idea of co-celebration in which all participants collectively express their unity in the priesthood on an equal level. The decline of the idea of silent concelebration, aided by an incorrect interpretation of a reply from the Holy Office in 1957, contributed to the development described above.

H. Schmidt criticized this tendency in Trier.[26] During the last two years several contributions appeared which marked genuine progress on precisely this point by studying the thought of the older authors in the light of the new sacramental theology, and thus made it possible to provide the right context for the declaration of Vatican Council II that concelebration is a manifestation of

---

*et apparenti unitate veram multiplicitatem ponat, in ipso autem sacramento conficiendo omnibus celebrantibus plane easdem partes concedat.* He repeated this in *Divinitas* 2 (1958), p. 254. Danneels and Tihon take this up again in the light of sacramental theology.

[24] Cf. J. Tillard, "Concélébration et messe communautaire," in *QLP* 43 (1962), pp. 22-35.

[25] N. Afanazieff (*Trapeza Gospodjna*, Paris 1952) thinks that the spoken concelebration is a clericalization of the eucharist because in his opinion the concelebrants turn away here from their original position of a participation based on the universal priesthood. Their position would somehow contradict the real nature of the eucharistic celebration (see the review in *OCP* 19, 1953, pp. 444-45). Although not a single Catholic author follows him to this extreme, he seems to me, all the same, to point to a tendency which may well be present in certain forms of concelebration.

[26] A survey of the Trier discussions may be found in *Heiliger Dienst* 17 (1963), pp. 64-8.

the unity of the priesthood.[27] These contributions[28] deserve a
little fuller treatment here. It is, therefore, proposed to devote
some space to a systematic discussion of concelebration in which
the thoughts of these authors will be integrated.

## II

### THE TERM "CONCELEBRATION"

Most authors, both old and recent, seem to agree that a
genuine concelebration of the eucharist presupposes the following conditions: a *principal celebrant,* a group or *"college"* of
*priests* functioning *as such*[29] which, under the *hierarchical* guidance of the principal celebrant, *celebrates* the eucharist *together
with him,* and does so *in the midst of the participating community.*

[27] *Constitution on the Sacred Liturgy,* article 57: "Concelebration,
whereby the unity of the priesthood is appropriately manifested . . ."

[28] G. Danneels, "Het probleem der concelebratie," in *CBG* 9 (1963),
pp. 160-89; P. Fransen, "Dogmatische beschouwingen over de concelebratie," in *TL* 47 (1963), pp. 337-62; P. Weber, "Eucharistie et ministère;
notes sur la concélébration," in *Coll. Mechl.* 48 (1963), pp. 449-72;
M. C. Vanhengel, "De celebrerende priester en de heiligende symboliek
der sacramenten," in *TT* 3 (1963), pp. 111-38; P. Tihon, "De la concélébration eucharistique," in *NRT* 96 (1964), pp. 579-607. The following studies of M. Nicolau, "La concelebración eucaristica," in *Salmanticenses* 8 (1961), p. 269; "Problemas del concilio vaticano II," in
*Vision teologica* (Madrid, 1963), pp. 139-72, and "La misa en la constitución liturgica del vaticano II," in *Salmanticenses* 11 (1964), pp. 276-82,
must be mentioned although they narrow down the theological problem
to the question about the unity or multiplicity of the sacrificial act. For
the more practical side of the question with which this article cannot deal,
I refer to commentaries on the Constitution such as: E. M. Lengeling,
*Die Konstitution des zweiten vatikanischer Konzils über die heutige
Liturgie. Lateinisch-deutscher Text mit einem Kommentar,* in the series
*Lebendiger Gottesdienst,* n. 5/6 (Münster, 1964), pp. 126-30; P.M.G(Y),
"La concélébration," in *LMD* 77 (1964), pp. 128-32; L. Brinkhoff,
"Hoofdstuk II. Over het hoogheilig mysterie van de eucharistie," in *TL*
48 (1964), pp. 131-32. As an introduction to the Constitution I must
add A. Nuij, "De concelebratie. Historische achtergronden van het con-
ciliebesluit," in *TL* 48 (1964), pp. 268-85 and F. Vandenbroucke, "Vers
un nouveau style de la messe," in *QLP* 45 (1964), pp. 143-49.

[29] When speaking of a "college of priests" I mean to include, *servatis
servandis,* a group of bishops or a group of bishops and priests. The case
of a single concelebrant I consider as a borderline case.

The principal celebrant acts as hierarchical leader and as the principle of the unity of the "college".[30] There are, however, some authors who feel themselves forced by the factual situation to add to this a broader definition. They give the name concelebration also to a more recent form, where all participating priests celebrate the eucharist on the same level, whether the community is present or not. H. Schmidt, who introduced the term "co-celebration" for this form, and Danneels point out that in this case one may ask how far this form realizes the full meaning of concelebration.

The outward form of concelebration has not always been the same in the Church, and even today there are differences in both East and West. Historians and theologians have found it rather difficult to give an exact description and an accurate theological assessment of these differences. For instance, it has not yet been possible even to find a satisfactory terminology to indicate the principal categories. Provisionally we opt for the distinction between *spoken* and *silent* concelebration. At the spoken concelebration the *whole* participating college of priests *pronounces* at least the *words of consecration together with* the principal celebrant (at co-celebration all the celebrants speak them collectively). At the silent concelebration the concelebrants do function as a college of priests in the celebration, but do *not* pronounce the words of consecration, which are pronounced by the principal celebrant only. A proper co-celebration is in this case not really possible.[31]

---

[30] This he can be either as hierarchical head of this community, or as host to, or guest of, the clergy or the bishop of other churches; or as delegated by the hierarchical head; or—and here the question becomes more difficult—as, in fact, the co-ordinator. Weber, *loc. cit.,* p. 553, draws attention to the difficulty of correctly interpreting the function of a bishop's "representative". As he points out, *loc. cit.,* pp. 565f., this is only possible because the one Spirit of the priestly ministry is given to the whole body.

[31] The distinction is inadequate. According to this, for instance, the consecration of an abbot is a silent concelebration, although the concelebrant says the whole of the canon, the words of the consecration excepted. But I prefer not to use Hanssens' terminology of *concelebratio sacramentalis* and *concelebratio caeremonialis* because, although the author

J. Hanssens had already asked in what sense both forms of concelebration did in fact consecrate. The question as put by him had become mainly historical, but in the nineteen-fifties it assumed practical importance and there arose a theological discussion. In this connection a distinction can be made of quite a different nature from the one put forward above, not primarily from the point of view of the outward form but from that of the effectiveness of the rite.[32] It is then possible to distinguish between a concelebration where the priests co-consecrate and a concelebration where they do not so co-consecrate. In the most recent ecclesiastical documents the former is also called *concelebratio valida*. Some authors speak of a *concelebratio confectionis* (*sc. sacramenti*) and a *concelebratio participationis*.[33]

According to a declaration of the Holy Office, the interpretation of which is a veritable *crux theologorum*, the silent concelebration at any rate is not co-consecratory today in the Western Church.[34] Some authors then drew the conclusion that it was forbidden.[35] Hürth and, recently, Nicolau have stressed that this conclusion is incorrect.[36] And this is true. The saying *"quod in-*

---

gave these terms a purely phenomenological use (cf. note 13), they were later tainted by theological implications which caused much confusion, doubtless against the author's intentions. For Hanssens' distinction between *concelebratio synaxalis* and *personalis*, see Tihon, *art. cit.*, p. 597.

[32] This discussion is only concerned with a very limited aspect of the effective nature of the eucharist: transubstantiation, with the "re-presentation" of Christ's sacrificial act linked with it according to certain theological opinions. In this connection it must be pointed out that the term "co-consecratory", used hereafter, is really incorrect because the consecration embraces far more than just transubstantiation.

[33] Danneels, *art. cit.*, p. 162, takes over this terminology from H. Schmidt, *Introductio*, p. 441, but it is not clear to me whether both authors use these terms in the same sense.

[34] *A.A.S.* 49 (1957), p. 370; *DS* 3928.

[35] *Lit. Wdb.*, p. 450.

[36] "Dubium non loquitur de *liceitate* vel *utilitate* atque *convenientia* concelebrationis caeremonialis, quae olim in sat frequenti usu fuisse dicitur, et quam . . . nonnulli Liturgistae, iique serii, hodie vellent repristinari" (F. Hürth, "Annotationes (super dubio "de valida concelebratione")," in *Periodica* 46 (1957), p. 249). M. Nicolau, in "La concelebración eucaristica," in *Salmanticenses* 8 (1961), p. 285, following him, observes: "By the reply of the Holy Office . . . silent concelebration is

*validum est illicitum"* does not apply here. According to Hürth, the intention of the Holy Office was to make it clear that at a silent concelebration (and, *a fortiori,* at a *messe communautaire*) only the principal celebrant consecrates.

Only if the total sense of concelebration were exclusively contained in co-consecration, the conclusion would be that silent concelebration is no longer of any value and therefore should cease to be practiced. That this is not the case is clear from H. Schmidt's excellent definition of this silent concelebration: *"est celebratio missae, in qua episcopus (aut unus sacerdos) consecrationem conficit, sed in qua tota communitas liturgica secundum suam structuram hierarchicam . . . agit ac participat modo visibili".*[37]

And with this we reach the problem of the theological meaning of concelebration.

## III

### THE MEANING OF CONCELEBRATION

The real theological problem is not the antiquated scholastic question of whether several priests can together pronounce the words of consecration validly.[38] Nor is it the question of whether only the spoken concelebration effects the consecration. This second question did indeed create a stir in the nineteen-fifties, as has been mentioned. But it was really prompted by a far too narrow view of both the nature of the eucharistic sacrament and the sacramental function of the priesthood. This view originated from the idea that the only strictly sacerdotal action at mass consisted in performing Christ's sacrificial act *in eiusdem persona.* Coupled with this was the theological theory that this sacrificial act lay in pronouncing the two formulae of consecration signify-

---

not forbidden. The Holy Office only declares against the suggestion that there is a valid co-consecration. But apart from this error, if we remain strictly within the limits of a mere ceremonial concelebration, nothing is said either against its liceity, utility or convenience."

[37] H. Schmidt, *Introductio,* p. 410.

[38] Cf. Nicolau, "La concelebración," etc., p. 287.

ing the separation of Body and Blood. The meaning of concelebration, implying a sacramental function of the college of priests, must then be wholly contained in the collective pronunciation of these formulae, as the *actio Christi se ipsum sacrificantis et offerentis*[39] can only then be performed by many, according to this view.

As indicated at the beginning of this article, there have been for some time tendencies in the theology of concelebration which did not limit its sacramental sense to the collective *confectio sacramenti* or to the collective performance of Christ's sacrificial act by a group of individual priests. From the beginning all informed authors have pointed out that the first sense of concelebration is that it is the *manifestation of the hierarchical unity of the Church*. The five recent authors, quoted in note 28, may be credited with having provided a sacramental basis for this statement. Most important here was a consistent application of the old ecclesial view of the sacrament as a celebration (*sacramentum est celebratio*).

All sacraments, including the eucharist, are actions of the Church. In such an action—here: the memorial celebration of the *Passio Domini* in its totality—God leads the Church to self-realization, and this self-realization takes place in the free, human, active cooperation in which she performs Christ's mystery through symbolic activity. This view, which does not deny but integrates the previous one, implies a much clearer perception of the hierarchical community (*synaxis*) as subject of the sacramental celebration. The whole community celebrates the *mysterium Passionis Domini,* but each member according to the function he has

---

[39] Thus, rightly, Pius XII in his allocution of September 22, 1956, in *A.A.S.* 48 (1956), p. 718 (cf. Schmidt, *Introductio,* p. 404). Note that the consecratory significance of the silent concelebration had already been for a long time the accepted opinion of several *auctores probati.* Both Hürth's interpretation (*art. cit.*) and Nicolau's ("La concelebración," etc. pp. 287-92) tend to interpret the Pope's "several" in this context as referring to several individual sacrificial acts (*i.e.,* "re-presentations" of Christ's sacrificial act). Nicolau thinks that there is a physical multiplicity of acts, but morally only one. Would this not imply that there is in fact a simultaneous celebration by many?

in the community as a whole. And this sheds special light on the sacramental position, in this celebration, of the college of those whose mission it is to serve the Body of the Church.[40] But then it becomes also possible to qualify the meaning of concelebration in a less univocal way and with finer nuances—it is no longer a question of "all or nothing".[41] We can now attempt a brief analysis of this sacramental function.

The eucharist is the sacrament in which the Church experiences the mystery of Christ in its fullness. It is therefore also the sacrament in which the unity of the Church becomes real in a communal and hierarchical celebration. And here concelebration—whether there is collective consecration or not is really of minor importance—plays an important part. For concelebration makes real the unity of the college of priests in the one Spirit of the ministry in the midst of the community for which their function was given. Each functionary, performing the sacramental task for which the Church ordained him, cooperates sacramentally with the bishop or his delegate as the center of this unity. And thus the unity of Christ's Body becomes manifest, as it must be manifested in the world.

Precisely because in this celebration the unity of priests and bishop becomes a sacramental reality, it is true, as Danneels said, that "the oneness of the principal celebrant is the norm for eucharistic celebration which adequately reflects the nature of the eucharist".[42] This perspective of the unity in the spirit of the

[40] The studies by Vanhengel and Weber are important contributions to this question.

[41] Tihon, art. cit., p. 600.

[42] Art. cit., p. 183. The following passage must be quoted: ". . . Christ is the chief celebrant who offers his sacrifice only within the unity of his Church, and her supreme power resides in the entire Ordo sacerdotalis as in her womb. The concelebrating presbyterium is then the manifestation within a definite ecclesiastical community of that Ordo, and the actualization, here and now, of this sacrificial power. For even when the priest functions alone . . . he can only perform an ecclesiastical symbolic action, doing this in virtue of Christ's priesthood insofar as this is present on earth in the entire Ordo sacerdotalis. Even as an isolated celebrant, the priest still functions as a member of a sacerdotal hierarchy and in virtue of powers possessed by that Ordo as a college. In concelebration, that which is always implied becomes explicit by signs: a

sacerdotal ministry, which all members of the priestly body share through the bishop and which empowers each priest individually to fulfil his mission, shows, according to Weber, that there is sense in the concelebration of newly ordained priests with their bishop. For they make this unity in the Spirit a concrete reality by celebrating with him at the moment when they are admitted to the college of priests and receive their mission from the bishop.[43] Before him, Franquesa had already pointed out how unity of faith and recognition of authority are implied in concelebration.[44]

This aspect of concelebration also brings out other aspects. When, for instance, bishops of various dioceses concelebrate in the presence of a community, it also shows that there is a bond between the various local Churches that make up the universal Church.[45] Thus concelebration is not only the realization of the internal unity of an individual community or Church, but also that of the communal nature of the universal Church in which all Churches share.[46] There is, therefore, also a good reason for various bishops concelebrating on the same level.

Both these aspects concur in a concelebration of pope and bishops. In this case one might say, it seems to me, that this con-

---

collegium of priests enters into the very sign of the eucharistic cele-bration, in order to support the activity of the chief celebrant" (*art. cit.,* p. 187).

[43] Weber, *art. cit.,* pp. 564-67. He rightly shows that for the priest the exercise of his eucharistic function in virtue of what he does means "in-volvement" and therefore sanctification. Tihon, *art. cit.,* p. 596, equally insists on this. The basis for these considerations which have broadened the understanding of the sanctifying efficacy of the eucharist, has been provided by Vanhengel in his outstanding study.

[44] A. Franquesa, "La concelebración—Nuevos testimonios?" in *Liturgica* (Montserrat, 1956), pp. 75-82.

[45] A. Franquesa, "La concélébration, rite de l'hospitalité ecclésiastique," in *ParLit.* 37 (1955), pp. 169-76; *id.,* "La concelebración. Nuevos testi-monios?" . . . pp. 82-6.

[46] Although what has been said shows that concelebration only achieves its full sacramental meaning when the whole community of God cele-brates the eucharist, there are, nevertheless, cases when it has meaning even when only clergy are present, *e.g.,* as the manifestation of brother-hood or solidarity in a religious community. Most authors point out rightly that a concelebration with a whole mass of priests would probably miss the point. But these things will only become clear in practice.

celebration, particularly when it takes place *in facie totius Ecclesiae,* even though by means of television, manifests and realizes the true unity of the college of bishops more clearly than one could ever express in a theoretical form.

There is no room to indulge in a study of the rite. Yet, one would like to point out, with various authors, that articles 57 and 58 of the Constitution on the Sacred Liturgy deal exclusively with concelebration insofar as it takes place with collective consecration. This means that silent concelebration, which remains licit, does not require the same complicated procedure prescribed by the Constitution for the rite with the collective consecration.[47]

[47] Thus M. Nicolau, "La misa en la constitución liturgica del vaticano II," in *Salmanticenses* 11 (1964), p. 277. See also F. Kolbe, "Die Liturgiekonstitution des Konzils: II. Praktische Hinweise," in *Lit. Jahrb.* 14 (1964), p. 128: "In article 57 concelebration is not expressly mentioned as sacramental. It is of course superfluous to state that the widely accepted practice of ceremonial concelebration still remains licit. Much is to be said in favor of not completely abandoning the practice at this time. In any case we may apply to silent concelebration what was said in the article, that 'Here the unity of the priesthood is suitably manifested'." For the rite, see A. Nuij, "Le rituel de la concélébration nouvelle," in *QLP* 45 (1964), pp. 206-27, and A. G. Martimort, "Le rituel de la concélébration," in *EL* 77 (1963), pp. 147-68.

# GODFRIED DANNEELS

Born June 4, 1933 in Kanegem, Belgium. He was ordained August 17, 1957 for the diocese of Bruges. He studied philosophy at the Institut Supérieur de Philosophie at the University of Louvain, and theology in Rome where he earned his doctorate in 1961 with the thesis, "L'acte de foi chez Henri de Gand". He is at present professor of sacramental theology and of liturgy at the seminary in Bruges. He has published several articles in the fields of theology and liturgy.

Godfried Danneels / *Bruges, Belgium*

# Communion under Both Kinds

I n article 55 of the Constitution on the Sacred Liturgy, Vatican Council II has re-introduced communion under both kinds for the faithful of the Western Church, at least in principle. Compared with the prevailing directives of canon law (Can. 852) this means a definite, though only disciplinary,[1] alteration in existing eucharistic practice. The question of the chalice for the laity has two aspects: on the one hand, it concerns a problem that has been aggravated in history by fierce controversies, and on the other, the granting or refusal of the chalice to the laity is bound to interest the theologian. A brief survey of the historical and theological implications of this issue might clarify certain points in the present situation of the Church.

I

### THE HISTORICAL DEVELOPMENT

For twelve centuries, communion under both kinds for all was the constant practice at the celebration of the eucharist in

---

[1] The Constitution mentions explicitly that this change in practice "in no way affects the dogmatic principles laid down by the Council of Trent" (Art. 55).

the West. It is true that communion under one kind was known in exceptional situations such as the communion of infants and of the sick, but the fact remains that lay access to the chalice was taken for granted in the Church at large. About 1200 A.D., however, a basic change took place in this practice: from that time on[2] communion took place only under the species of bread. The motives that brought about this development were doubtless manifold and of different kinds.[3] The worry about reverent handling of the eucharist, particularly in the use of the chalice (*periculum effusionis*) and already observable in the early days of the Church,[4] reached a climax at that time. It was strengthened by the growing realism inspired by the *theology of the real presence,* typical of that period.

Practical considerations and the pastoral usefulness of communion under one kind also influenced the issue. Yet, the objection based on hygiene and the great number of communicants, rather prominent in our days, seem to have been of little consequence at that time. The principal argument for the change in the communion rite was perhaps the theology of the period which stressed that the whole Christ was totally present under either species (Thomas Aquinas, *Summa Theol.,* III, q.76, a. 2-3; q.80, a. 12). This teaching of concomitance which provided a theological guarantee that non-use of the chalice implied no essential diminution of sacramental grace, eliminated the last arguments for the retention of communion under both kinds. From that time on, lay communion under one kind became as tranquilly accepted as communion under both kinds had been until then.

From the 15th century onward, however, the chalice for the laity became a bone of contention in religious polemics. Heterodox groups, such as the Hussites (Utraquists, Calixtines) made

[2] St. Thomas, however, mentions some Churches (*in quibusdam ecclesiis*) where the practice of communion under both kinds still prevailed (*Summa Theol.,* III, q. 80, a. 12).

[3] For this, see particularly the study by J. J. Megivern, *Concomitance and Communion,* referred to below.

[4] G. Dix, *The Treatise on the Apostolic Tradition of Saint Hippolytus of Rome* (London, 1937), p. 59; J. Jungmann, *Missarum Sollemnia* (Vienna: Herder, 1948), Vol. II, pp. 464-68.

the chalice the symbol of their opposition to Rome. Those groups did not only use communion under both kinds as the rite by which they distinguished themselves from Rome, but also—and this was wholly new—as the sharp edge of their theological position: they supported their accusation of Rome by John 6, 53: "Unless you eat the flesh of the Son of man and drink his blood, you have no life in you." After a first condemnation at the Council of Constance (1415) and many further complications, the chalice was finally conceded to Bohemia by the Compactata of Prague (1433). But Pius II cancelled this concession again in 1462. Many returned to the Roman practice but, later on, others joined the Lutheran Reformation where the conflict about the chalice broke out afresh. It was again John 6, 53 which loomed large in the popular preaching of Reformers and even perturbed Catholics. Many among these asked for the chalice in order to deprive the Reformation of a powerful weapon.

The attitude of the Council of Trent was, on the one hand, uncompromising insofar as the dogmatic background of the controversy was concerned, but on the other it was hopelessly hesitant and divided about the practical point of granting or withholding the chalice. No grace essential for salvation was lost by those who received communion under one kind only (Denz. 929-937), but, granted that point, the Council at first did not even wish to decide whether it was opportune to yield to the demands of the emperor and the faithful and to re-introduce the chalice. The issue was tackled only after repeated insistence by the emperor's legates and the pope. When the papal legates foresaw that there would be no satisfactory majority for the chalice in the confused debate ("ce débat scabreux, qui avait failli mettre l'assemblée sens dessus dessous," said the bishop of Zara,[5]) they decided to put to the vote the proposal to leave the whole issue to the pastoral judgment of the pope. A vast majority agreed at once, obviously relieved after unpleasant debates. On April 16, 1564, Pius IV granted the chalice to the metropolitans of Cologne, Mainz, Trier, Salzburg and Gran. But one after the other these concessions were

[5] Hefele-Leclercq, *Histoire des Conciles*, IX, 2, p. 717.

revoked: the chalice had become the confessional symbol of the Reformation and was rejected even by those Catholics to whom it had been granted.[6]

## II

### THE THEOLOGICAL RICHES OF THE CHALICE[7]

In spite of all theological justification of communion under one kind one cannot deny that it demands considerable ingeniousness to cope with John 6, 53: after all, communion under one kind requires proof of a theological nature and the direct meaning of Christ's words indicates communion under both kinds. Moreover,

[6] For the historical development and abandonment of the chalice for the laity the following studies will be useful: A. Franzen and K. Rahner, "Laienkelchbewegung," in *LexThK*, VI, col. 744-46; G. Constant, *Concession à l'Allemagne de la communion sous les deux espèces par Pie IV*, 2 vols. (Paris, 1922-1926); A. Franzen, *Die Kelchbewegung am Niederrhein im 16. Jahrhundert* (Münster, 1955); R. Schreiber, "Der Kampf um den Laienkelch," in *Zeitschr. f. südetendeutsche Geschichte*, I, pp. 95-122; H. Lutz, "Bayern und der Laienkelch," in *Quellen und Forschungen aus italienischen Archiven und Bibliotheken* 34 (1954), pp. 203-35; G. Schwaiger, "J. A. Möhler und der Laienkelch," in *Pro Mundi Vita. Festschrift der Theol. Fak. München* (1960), pp. 82-96; K. Amon, "Calicem salutaris accipiam. Beiträge zur Geschichte der Utraquistischen Gründonnerstagkommunion in Deutschland," in *Heiliger Dienst* 12 (1963), pp. 16-26; G. Danneels, "De Lekenkelk," in *Tijdschr. v. Lit.* 46 (1962), pp. 181-191; *id.*, "Het Vol-teken van de eucharistische maaltijd. De lekenkelk," *ibid.* 47 (1963), pp. 363-81. This last article contains a fuller bibliography on p. 374, n. 31.

[7] For the theological problems connected with the chalice for the laity, see E. Dublanchy, "Communion sous les deux espèces," in *Dict. Theol. Cath.* III (1923), col. 552-72; J. Quasten, "Sobria ebrietas in Ambrosius, De Sacramentis," in *Misc. Mohlberg* I (1948), pp. 117-25; H. Schürmann, "Das apostolische Interesse am eucharistischen Kelch," in *Münch. Theol. Zeitschr.* 4 (1953), pp. 223-31; J. Pascher, "Der Kelch in den Texten der römischen Messliturgie," in *Lit. Jahrb.* 10 (1960), pp. 217-26; M. Lipps, "Brot und Wein. Das Sakrament in beiden Gestalten," in *Hochland* 53 (1961), pp. 293-302; J. J. Megivern, *Concomitance and Communion. A Study in Eucharistic Doctrine and Practice* (Freiburg, S., Univ. Press, 1963); B. Vanbilsen, "De Lekenkelk," in *De Nieuwe Mens* 15 (1963-4), pp. 207-13; T. Wilmering, "Brood en Wijn. Sacrament van de twee gedaanten," in *Streven* 16, pp. 311-18; J. J. Megivern, "Communion under both species," in *Worship* 37 (1962-3), pp. 50-58; A. Michel, "Communion sous les deux espèces. Comment concilier la pratique de la communion sous une seule espèce avec les textes de saint Jean. Histoire de cette pratique," in *L'Ami du Clergé* 72 (1962), pp. 701-3.

communion under one kind brings about a noticeable impoverish-
ment on the level of the sign. The solemn eucharistic sign of
the biblical meal is reduced to a shrunken rite. This impoverish-
ment may not take place where the cause of the eucharistic grace
operates, but it shows more plainly and eloquently on the level of
the sign.

Now, no one will deny the catechetical and kerygmatic importance of the sacramental sign because this determines in large
measure the way in which the recipient assimilates sacramental
grace in faith. The administration of a sacrament must not only
make sure of the *opus operatum,* but it must also create that concrete atmosphere of faith that will provide the recipient with the
maximum assistance in the discharge of *his* contribution to the
sacrament, namely, the *opus operans.* And this concrete atmosphere of faith depends a great deal upon the sign.

That is why it is wholly desirable that, apart from cases where
it is impossible or creates serious difficulties, both celebrant and
people receive the sacrament in the fullness of the sign. This not
only ensures an outward and faithful correspondence to the nar-
rative of the institution but will bring out to the full a whole series
of biblical and theological values, both in connection with the
sign at the consecration and the sign at the communion, the
*manducatio.* I enumerate only a few:[8] the festive character of the
biblical meal is not expressed in the eating of the bread but in the
drinking of the wine (Ps. 104, 15; Ps. 23, 5; Judges 9, 13; Prov-
erbs 9, 2); the allusion to the Jewish Passover where the drink
was spaced out and every drink was accompanied by a brief explanation (1 Cor. 10, 16); the eschatological significance of the
cup at the last supper (Mark 14, 25; Luke 22, 16. 18) and of
"drinking the cup . . . until he comes" (1 Cor. 11, 26).

Finally there is the allusion to the blood of the Mount Sinai
covenant, with which all were sprinkled (Ex. 24, 8) and the allusion to the Ebed Jahweh theology whose blood was "poured out

[8] For a more extensive treatment of the theological themes connected
with the chalice, see G. Danneels, "Het Vol-teken van de eucharistische
maaltijd. De Lekenkelk," in *Tijdschr. v. Lit.* 47 (1963), pp. 363ff.

for all" (Is. 53, 12), which are both linked with the cup. All these catechetical elements that are supposed to form and to stimulate the living faith lose half their value when they remain confined to the "sign" of the consecration. Only when the whole community actually shares the chalice can the recipient's personal participation be expressed in a satisfactorily "significant" way.

Now that the communion of the chalice has been cleared of its polemic overload, it assumes outstanding ecumenical significance.[9] Protestant and Eastern Churches will appreciate this profoundly. Moreover, this ecumenical joy may well inspire the wisdom and courage that will be required to clear up some practical objections (such as hygiene and the time factor) that are necessarily bound up with this full expression of the eucharistic sacramental sign.

[9] For all this, see J. Lescrauwaet, "Katholieke liturgiehervorming en reformatorisch getuigenis," in *Tijdschr. v. Lit.* 47 (1963), pp. 313-15.

# PART III

DO-C DOCUMENTATION
CONCILIUM

## ROSARIO SCARPATI

Born May 22, 1930 in Sorrento, Italy, he was ordained in 1952 for the Diocese of Sorrento. He earned degrees in philosophy and theology with the thesis, "La dottrina della predestinazione nel pensiero di Tommaso Campanella". His published works include *L'evoluzione del comportamento in un processo di sviluppo* (1962), and *Problemi sociali e culturali dello sviluppo* (1963), in addition to a number of other articles in the sociological field. In his many published works he devotes himself especially to the problems of economic development and socio-religious integration. At present he is a professor of history and philosophy, consultor in sociology, and director of research for FERES.

Rosario Scarpati / *Sorrento, Italy*

# Evolution of the Concept of Economic Expansion

## INTRODUCTION

The term "economic expansion" has become a magic phrase, almost a myth continuously revived in every debate concerning socio-economic politics. At times it seems that such a term and its related word, "underdevelopment", could and should sum up or even condition every judgment on the future of a people's civilization. In recent years thoroughgoing changes have succeeded one another at an ever-increasing pace. Moreover, all the sciences, above all, the experimental ones, concerned with grasping and analyzing constants in the transformations themselves, somehow have had to change their object or their point of view and method of observation. In fact, one has only to think of the value given at present to the dynamics of economic and natural sciences, or of the time factor which is by now the basis of the technical implications and applications of the theories of relativity.

The increasing interest concerning economic expansion has been extended to a series of humanity's historical experiences since the beginning of this century. And this is true first of all because the phenomenon of underdevelopment has appeared as an imposing and tragic exception in the process of expansion affecting some economic systems—an expansion brought about first by the thrust of colonialism, and then by the necessity of preserving the high standards of productivity which the new technology had imposed. Inasmuch as it affected the survival of two-thirds of mankind, such a phenomenon could no longer be set aside in accordance with the traditional theory, even if some fundamental categories pertinent to this theory were to be jeopardized. War, in turn, though increasingly recognized as a useless carnage by all, has abundantly demonstrated that it is possible to solve the problems of scientific organization related to production by means of political action aiming at the complete exploitation of natural resources and manpower; and, hence, it has demonstrated that the task to be historically pursued by those entrusted with the destiny of people does not consist so much in finding means to the end as in defining the ends themselves.

Finally, a collective consciousness regarding this idea of growth has affirmed itself in the form of human progress toward an *ideal* beyond history, or as history's final goal. Such consciousness is collective in that it is not so much the fruit of knowledge brought about by the philosophy of the enlightenment, as it is the outcome of a *social awareness*. In fact, within the latter, man has been able to discover—through his dominion over nature which he exerts in union with others—the determining weight of the group, the mass, the great dimensions, the attitudes and ideas of the community. For this reason all the resurgent messianic doctrines appear to be not so much the collective projection of individual utopias, as it had been in the past, but rather an historical outcome of the experiences shared in common in the technological world. And such experiences are directly realized within cultural areas endowed with richer resources and inventiveness, or else they are learned through communication whereby a constant intercouse between person and person, people and people, is assured.

However, we would depart from truth if we failed to underline the fact that this consciousness of the realities promoting an interest in economic expansion has also brought to light the latter's profound ambiguities. In fact, we note that the definition of indexes, factors and causes affecting economic expansion—that is, the theoretical definition of those elements allowing us to understand economic expansion so that we may, in practice, promote and direct it—is still uncertain, confused and even sometimes contradictory. The ever-growing complexity of structural forms in the various societies has contributed to doing away with all deterministic explanations, while implementing the search for different factors and causes which, however, delay the answers as they complicate the questions.

In the recent past, nonetheless, an attempt was made to give a univocal and clear answer, but the results have been scanty. Thus, we can envisage three directions of thought, even if they have no sufficient integration:

1. Some thinkers have utilized the term "economic development" only to point to certain direct and specific changes that affect the various aspects of structure or of socio-economic dynamics (industrialization, agrarian reform, cultural modernization, etc.). Thus, such changes would only represent the tactical or crucial stage within a really global and harmonious development of society, the definition of which is carefully avoided.

2. Others have focused their attention on long-term objectives that have a global character within the growth-process. They have, in other words, attempted to point out some goals toward which the evolution of a society, which they consider to be a complex and historically determined organism, must converge. In this category fall all the disputes on uniform planning, as well as the actual plan and the values that are to guide the elaboration and realization of this total goal beyond the purely technical stage.

3. Others, at a completely different level, have tried to grasp in every economic growth-process the ultimate meaning of human history rising again by means of value-judgments and a well-

defined philosophical perspective to what is the ultimate principle of all historical processes and, finally, to a philosophy or theology of history. In this category fall all talk of cultural nationalism, imperialism, and what we might call applied Teilhardism, etc.

The Church, as a People of God on the march, is coextensive with economic expansion inasmuch as the latter represents a particular stage in human experience and consciousness. Whatever is human is not foreign to the Church; her presence in the world does not add to her history, for she represents, with regard to it, but a greater level of consciousness and a clear eschatological vision. The Church *must* then have an interest in it and pass judgment on the strategy of growth, on its historical goals and on its meaning, as much as she *must* share an interest in every leavening agent which affects the human dough as it strives to achieve a higher stage of life and action. In this respect, the Church holds an irreplaceable role within growth.

For her to play such a role, it is necessary to analyze: (a) which factors intervene in economic evolution and what their relationships and interdependences are; (b) what influence is exerted by such factors at the level of individual as well as group-consciousness, in order to determine this growth-action within a society; and (c) which means of action enhance or accelerate an orderly economic expansion, as we take into account the intervening factors and their influence.

The questions confronting the Church, in a drastic or, at times, alternative way, concern, above all, those historical situations wherein the economic growth-process has not yet begun or is just on its way. It is always very important to know in such cases how to read the signs of the age in order not to betray the mandate of Christ and the expectations of the world.

## THE CONCEPT OF ECONOMIC EXPANSION

Before facing, more directly, the Church and growth argument, one must briefly analyze the evolution of the very concept of economic expansion in recent years. It is a well-known fact that the very existential conditions wherein some theories were elaborated have undoubtedly changed; and that human experience (already mentioned above) has brought to a state of crisis, at the historical and mental level, all that man believed he had acquired once and for all. Thus, a first observation is suggested by the everyday usage of the word expansion, which in fact indicates an advancement toward the *ideal,* and which in turn ceases when such an *ideal term* has been attained. If we take man as an example, we hold his growth to be his advancement toward the highest point of his stature, strength, capacity of action, intellectual maturity and moral life.

However, it is already apparent that insofar as man is concerned there exists no *ideal* in an absolute sense, for the complexity of his body and of his psyche brings to light the fact that only relative and successive goals exist for him. This means that the growth-concept is already complex with respect to the individual man. Moreover, such a concept becomes more complex if we consider the individual as being historically a part of social organisms (family, groups, Churches, States). We must then take into account all the notions drawn by human experience from the long compliance with, and codification of, the laws regulating the static and dynamic social structure. If we proceed, therefore, from the complex concept of economic expansion as suggested by daily observation, we can already distinguish two ways of understanding this concept: mechanical and organic. As regards the former, the ends (or *the ideal*) are of a quantitative order, and they can be determined beforehand and also attained with certainty, for they are necessarily bound to times and means that can be scientifically verified.

This basic dualism, which also responds to a general attitude in regard to life and history, explains the confusion in present-day literature related to economic expansion. There, in fact, one can note the use of expressions by which meanings that actually have a wider scope are ambiguously minimized, while other partial expressions, having by definition only a methodological meaning, are magnified. Undoubtedly, it can be stated that the organic concept of development has proved to be the most valid and that it has certainly made this term very popular in the literature devoted to collective aspirations. At present, the term "economic expansion" does not take in only one aspect of reality, even if it be the economic one, because the experience of humanity has hastened the integration of diverse disciplines by exposing the naiveté of those scholars who were intent upon formulating an abstract science that would have a universal application. Hence arises the necessity of taking into account the ever-increasing number of factors, so that one is able afterward to identify in a concrete manner those orientations that favor an orderly and continuous growth; and this is what is meant by organic economic growth.[1]

However, to what can we attribute this substantial change in the concept of growth particularly with respect to the economic thought that brought about its initial and fundamental success? The word "growth" has appeared in the terminology of economics as a special expression of the dynamic theory. Dynamic theory is an economic doctrine wherein time is considered to be an essential factor. This is due to the fact that time is considered as the variable on which depend different economic quantities. In the theory of economic development, the essential character of time changes qualitatively. "Time is viewed as the dimension in which a human activity (human in the real sense of the word) takes place; that is, an activity that creates a sequence of events, each of which is qualitatively new and irreducible to the preceding ones. Hence, this is an activity which in the course of time

---

[1] B. F. Hoselitz, (Ed.) *The Progress of Underdeveloped Areas* (The Univ. of Chicago Press, 1952): "When people study economic and technological growth they cannot understand the ultimate determinants of its process unless the line of demarcation between economics and social anthropology is broken." R. W. Goldsmith, *The Comparative Study of Economic Growth and Structure* (National Bureau of Economic Research, New York), p. 85: "Economists and statisticians who work on the economic development problem must conclude that the ensemble of the measurable economic facts called by them 'growth' are closely bound with and influenced by, the non-economic factor."

produces processes characterized not simply by the variation of determinate quantities, but essentially by the movements toward new positions that are always qualitatively different." [2]

Economists, not so long ago, used to elaborate their theories in a world in which the time factor was not integrated in the economic analysis: in a world lacking true temporality. The *homo oeconomicus* considered himself to be endowed with a perfect rationality and would move in an eternal present.[3] Classical economists, on the other hand, had reduced every developmental analysis to the study of a progression toward the state of equilibrium. Although accepting the distinction, which was formulated later on, between the short-term and the long-term period, they set aside the problem of change from one period to another (along with the problems inherent in the relationships that determine the structural changes in growth) in order to uphold the elements on which the abstract notion of equilibrium used to depend. As regards the very long-term period (during which take place the "movements brought about by the gradual development of technological know-how, population, capital and . . . the changing conditions on which supply and demand depend from generation to generation"),[4] it is easy to understand how its characteristics made it foreign to economic analysis.[5] Confined to such a period, economic expansion did not seem to be the object of a scientific analysis.[6]

In this way, economic analysis refused, in its rigorous logic, the pressure coming from social forces or from the many social questions, and thus it inevitably oriented itself toward efficiency-science, which held as foreign those variables peculiar to man

[2] C. Napoleoni, *Dizionario di Economia politica* (Milan, 1956), p. 1556.

[3] Cf. R. Barre, *La Période dans l'analyse économique* (Paris, 1950), p. 15.

[4] Cf. A. Marshall, *Principles of Economics* (Macmillan, New York, 1922), p. 71.

[5] Cf. L. Robbins, *An Essay on the Nature and Significance of Economic Science* (London, 1935).

[6] Cf. H. Guitton, "Oscillation et Croissance," in *Economie appliquée* (Jan.-June 1954), pp. 178-206.

(whether it was a matter of an individual or of a group) and not reducible to, or compatible with, quantities that can be analyzed by means of a rational method. Always more attractive, partiality was accepted as a starting and as a reference point in the study of social behavior so as to assure the logical rigor of the discipline along with discarding utopias.

Thus, with Marx and Schumpeter, the problem of organic growth is directly or indirectly faced through the introduction of variables heretofore neglected or considered not subject to economic analysis. This introduction of new elements—to which there will be added, later, some variations emanating from the historical context, political experience and "mental universes"— has in more recent times prompted the gradual passage from economic theory to growth theory.

It must be observed, however, that the Marxist theory faces the problem of economic development by focusing on capitalism. And while remaining, on account of the importance attached to the accumulation of capital, very close to classical thought, it fundamentally departs from it, for it considers accumulation nothing but a variable dependent on sociological factors.[7] In fact, the economic growth-process is for Marx founded on the behavior and strategy of a social group, and it implies in its development a transformation of sociological data affecting production. The power of entrepreneurs over the economy and society on account of their private ownership of the means of production is on the one hand a cause preventing harmonious growth and, on the other, the foundation of its dynamism. The accumulation of individual and social capital depends on the capitalization of the profit-value, which is closely bound to the behavior of capitalist entrepreneurs as well as to the pertinent institutional framework.

Economic growth takes place only in a sociologically stable environment. As the growth-process is realized, the environment is

---

[7] Cf. E. Mosse, *Marx et le problème de la croissance dans une économie capitaliste* (Paris, 1956).

modified and this modification reacts, in turn, on the growth-process itself. Thus, Marxist theory demonstrates the fundamental importance which sociological and institutional factors have within a balanced economic growth. By introducing an endogenous factor, namely, the tendency to lower profit, the Marxist economic principle explains the arrest of capitalistic growth and the collapse of the State. In conclusion, it can be said that upon emphasizing the importance of sociological factors within a growth-process, the Marxist theory has denied the spontaneous equilibrium, even if it has formulated a series of categories which at present cannot withstand scientific criticism. Thus, in the presence of problems regarding underdevelopment, Marxist theory has been unable to foresee the logic of other factors, and so it has only applied a seemingly rigid and abstract scheme outside the historical context that occasioned it.

Schumpeter maintains a keen sense of the dimensions affecting economic growth, as it seeks openings in which to insert the direct action of man. The idea of innovation is the central point in Schumpeter's vision. His analysis proceeds from the determination that the circular flow, which represents a situation of equilibrium, "is nothing but an abstract construction trying to make a cliché out of the consequences of a limited number of economic forces that are very real." [8] These forces may have, instead, an external origin (physical, political, institutional data) or be partially economic (the number of men and their distribution by age). The growth-factor is identified with an element to be found within the system, the manifestation of which is unforeseeable: the *innovation*. This innovation is intrinsic in the system, for it acts upon the production-data combination, whatever its form may be: new products, new energy, new method, new market, new organization of industry. "*Ex post*, its endogenous character is always perceived. *Ex ante*, it cannot be perceived with our analytical apparatus; nor can we count with

[8] J. Schumpeter, "Explanations on the Business Cycles," in *Economics* (1927), p. 290.

absolute certainty on its coming into being." [9] Once it has come in sight, innovation upsets the system and gives rise to a "creative destruction" whereby old relationships and old structures are torn down.

In conclusion, Schumpeter discovers man's direct responsibility in growth, because the innovator and dynamic entrepreneur, though being such because of his bond with the technological factor which is the true and proper field of innovation, is always, to say the least, the expression of a society or of a series of social habits. Following the main lines of Schumpeter's theory, it is therefore easy to proceed to the analysis of the sociocultural environment characterizing innovation, otherwise unjustifiable in its original and creative value.

Even if elaborated with the framework of our Western mentality, these two briefly examined sample analyses indicate how some traces, which are important for a more coherent and concrete discourse on the dynamics of economic expansion, were the patrimony of economic thought. Such traces were not followed up at first, and when a reference was made to them in more recent times, historical experience discovered not only their validity but also their limitations. Notwithstanding the fact that they were dynamic, they were not able in fact to embrace all the factors that were evident through the phenomenon of *underdevelopment*.

As we said in the introduction, it is this very phenomenon that has brought the theory of economic growth to a state of crisis. In order to begin the discussion on the concept of underdevelopment correctly, one must avoid the mistaken perspective of those who envisage a twofold reality: one frantically in motion, the other totally static. This error is usually made by those who confine themselves to an economic terminology. One must instead recognize (in a preliminary manner) the existence of a dynamism peculiar to underdeveloped societies which stands out even more when the latter are compared with developed societies, and raises problems of a completely different nature

[9] *Ibid.*, p. 292.

in the area of political knowledge and action. The structures of the compared economic and social systems must therefore be regarded as *dynamic* even if we grant them an intrinsic "margin of autonomy" [10] as well as, in consequence, a profound differentiation in the manner in which they operate and evolve. This preliminary observation must be thoroughly examined.

The dynamism of underdeveloped societies does not appear to be directly conditioned by an aspiration to an ever-growing possession of material goods, and it does not necessarily move ahead according to the patterns followed by industrialized societies. The transforming powers, remarks Balandier, do not always aim at the betterment of material conditions of life, for well-being is not always their objective. The solution of problems arising from the state of underdevelopment requires a particular readjustment of internal dynamism. This is almost impossible without an ideological transformation that is capable of inserting sociological agents into new orbits, since depression often forces even ideals into a state of passive fatalism. This spiritual readiness is made more urgent by the rhythm of sociological and technological change. In fact, the spreading of new methods of production; the reversal in the play of forces from within, and, outwardly, with respect to traditional economies; the tendency to individualize both revenues and utilization of wealth; the rise of the competitive function in relations of pure exchange and reciprocity; the transformation of social functions and of socio-cultural environments—all this imposes, as a matter of fact, unavoidable choices while the rhythm of individual and social life must be adjusted to new esthetical, ethical and logical models.[11]

Now every outside intervention into an underdeveloped zone becomes a real dilemma. As a result, the very conception of economic expansion is deeply conditioned. Technological effi-

[10] Cf. P. A. Sorokin, *Society, Culture and Personality: Their Structure and Dynamics* (New York, 1947), pp. 332-35; 643-45; *Id., Social and Cultural Dynamics* (American Book Co., New York, 1957), pp. 630-46.

[11] "Le contexte socio-culturel et le coût social du progrès," in *Le Tiers Monde* (Paris, 1956), pp. 289-303.

ciency, rationality and positiveness in the structure and culture of industrialized societies—all this runs up against the skepticism of underdeveloped societies where ethics and values are concerned. If the structures and forms of developed societies represent a result of the reciprocal influence of the two factors, how can one be established without the other? Is growth necessarily bound up, in its common significance, with the concept of well-being as this is understood by some Western societies, since the sociological aspect of economic growth seems to find its natural completion in connection with human needs and their gratification?

Let us consider, as an example, the innovating function that Schumpeter envisaged as the flywheel of growth:

"The problem of economic growth related to the areas outside the capitalistic markets is . . . that of creating a productive system sufficiently integrated *in a short time* rather than gradually, as was the case with those economies which, during the 19th century, became industrialized by stages. Actually, the problem originates from the fact that, while in already industrialized countries the *ex post* coordination of investments must take place through the *increments* of productive capacity and involves a relatively modest share of the national capital, in countries where the industrialization process is just beginning, this coordination must instead take place through *initial* investments, each of which is a relevant share of the still modest national capital. Since this is the picture within which decisions to invest are to be arrived at in underdeveloped countries, that often-repeated remark seems to be unjustified (provided it is based on this circumstance alone) which holds that the industrialization processes are unlikely to take place in those countries because they do not sufficiently possess the categories once present in, and favorable to, the industrialization of the countries now developed.

"Enterpreneurs, and those who are likely to become such, find themselves making decisions on investments in underdeveloped countries in circumstances totally different from those surrounding the pioneers of the first industries. The picture indeed differs because of the increase of difficulties in modern technological procedures and because of the competition encountered by the newly developed countries in the markets on which they must operate. And we cannot see any ground for the belief that the creators of the first industries could repeat their undoubtedly great experience in an underdeveloped country if this were simply able to offer them the institutional framework in which they successfully operated in their time." [12]

Hence, the global, extremely rapid, rigidly technical character of the intervention in underdeveloped areas for the purpose of starting the growth-process calls for new approaches in an economic picture other than that characteristic of developed societies.

It is for this and other reasons that prominent economists hold: "Economic analysis, if it is to be realistic, must deal with all the relevant factors; the general economic theory must become social theory." [13] "After Adam Smith, works on political economy have developed the idea that consumption is the only end of production, but in actual life this concept has never played an essential role. The essential objective was production in view of immediate profits while this production was not at all the basic preoccupation of the State . . . Any parliamentary document picked at random in any developed country, during this initial period of industrialization, will reveal a terminology as well as an ideology totally different from the terminology and ideology that nowadays characterize the growth of underdeveloped countries." [14]

A national and political effort tending to favor economic growth is a phenomenon new to the historical scene. Since the national action constantly aims at bettering standards of living, the choice of methods to realize this end is limited to the exist-

[12] P. Saraceno, *Iniziativa privata e azione pubblica nei piani di sviluppo economico* (Rome, 1959), pp. 13-14.

[13] G. Myrdal, *Teoria Economica e paesi sottosviluppati* (Milan, 1959), p. 129.

[14] G. Myrdal, *Une Economie Internationale* (Paris, 1958), pp. 225-26.

ing methods of growth—over and above the related established means—and they all become simple means toward the end. Thus, however, the problem of growth is not reduced to one of economic technology. The addition of specific methods or the assimilation of methods tested elsewhere cannot substitute for a global vision of the economy nor of a society where growth is beginning or is being encouraged. Consequently, the choice of methods to be followed is inevitably influenced by political, ideological and social factors that emphasize or minimize the seriousness of the need.

From another point of view, the evaluation of the initial stage of economic growth, when relations among different economies have been established, is often upset by the periods of change that destroy the residues of politico-historical order and accelerate their decomposition. The traditional theory proves inadequate to offset the resulting imbalance. The latter was never interested in problems wherein a marked difference exists between the various methods of production, corresponding to highly important differences in the relative rarity of factors, as they also correspond to huge differences in the living standards within the socio-cultural system, and, particularly, within the institutional framework. This, actually, is due to the fact that, even though the traditional theory admitted the existence of two orders, economic and non-economic, it always held that only the former could rationally be analyzed in their interrelations. Now Myrdal holds: "It is precisely within the realm of this large section of the social sphere neglected by economic analysis in its abstraction from the *non-economic factors,* that the assumed balance lacks stability. These non-economic factors cannot be considered as static data; when they act, their reaction is normally one of imbalance." [15] The conclusion to be drawn is evident.

If other non-economic factors—administrative efficiency, sanitary situation, degree of education, stimulants to action, causes motivating behavior—must be invoked (besides those recog-

---

[15] G. Myrdal, *Teoria Economica e paesi sottosviluppati,* p. 21.

nized as economic by the traditional theory) in order to render intelligible the economic growth-process in an underdeveloped country, the specific character of the science of economics is likely to be extended too far, even to the point of its breaking into a different type of analysis which, in a wide sense, can be called sociological. One cannot, therefore, assume a process of growth based only on the economy. The rethinking of economic theory under the stimulant of underdevelopment has been accelerated by a series of factors on the historical plane:

(a) The growing political importance of underdeveloped countries, with the rise of nationalism, and the insertion, more or less marked at the ideological level, of the "third world" in the dialectic of blocks;

(b) the failure of technical assistance destined for many underdeveloped countries, due to lack of consideration of the characteristics peculiar to the society for whose benefit the intervention was meant, and especially of its sociocultural preparedness for technical intervention;

(c) the necessity of innovating without disintegrating the traditional values that regulate and direct the social life of the community marked for intervention, lest the intervention itself become a failure;

(d) the ever-growing necessity of having the national and local communities participate in the process of economic expansion in order to insure the organic promotion of all their members at the civilian level;

(e) the necessity of avoiding political upheavals (capable of subverting the entire setup of social forces) and of taking into account the ideological components and the institutional picture in which such forces express themselves and oppose one another;

(f) the ever-growing tendency in all underdeveloped countries to formulate long-range plans which give rise to huge problems at the level of personnel and of cultural organization in general.

Under the impulse of all these factors, the literature on economic growth has enriched itself with a series of studies on the social and cultural aspects of economic development; in turn, a critical analysis of the activity performed on the international political level has yielded further results of an operational order. Research has therefore been undertaken in order to pinpoint the socio-cultural problems connected with the change, or the obstacles to the change, represented by social structures or by cultural values that are present in various societies. Such research has led to the identification of a sociocultural world (autonomous to a certain extent or subject to laws of a different nature) which surrounds and influences economic decisions themselves and may jeopardize their effectiveness.

Thus the theory of underdevelopment, far from being a rehash of the growth theory, has proved to be a theory on the intercultural influences among societies at different technical levels; a theory which studies the specific socio-cultural changes resulting from their contacts.[16]

Thus, the way has been cleared for considerations on the system of values that may resist change; and this happens for the difficulties encountered by instrumental technology upon being introduced in underdeveloped societies; difficulties that are recognized *a priori* as originating from attitudes or motivations of individuals and groups constantly referring themselves to a scale of values. Any growth-promoting action risks failure upon intervention, unless there is an introduction of new values in the existing socio-cultural context. It is not a matter of replacing the existing attitudes with others—the literature on the subject adds, in a concluding way—but rather one of being able to check their effects (functional or disfunctional as they may be) and the connection existing between certain attitudes and certain motivations structurally and dynamically integrated in social life. This is due to the fact that these very attitudes and

---

[16] H. Janne, *Changements techniques, economiques et sociaux* (Paris, 1958), p. 71: "Underdevelopment is a notion or rather a problem originating from the interaction among societies at different technical levels, in a world in which the question of the technical equipment of the collectivities occupies first place among those posed by the industrial revolution."

motivations—including those referring to economic activity—
may be functional or disfunctional with regard to growth, according to the socio-cultural context in which they act and
according to the process originating them in individual and social habits.[17]

As a final result, that so-called "Western ethnocentrism"—
according to which economic expansion, where accepted in
theory, was viewed prevalently as an extension or application of
what was thought to be the superior Western model—has been
abandoned. It has been realized that, rather, one has to analyze
the factors determining the change (according to the societies
in which the intervention is taking place) and, jointly, the content, the means and the periods of cultural modernization. Another series of studies has thus been added to the previous one
on the innovating incidence of entrepreneurs, on the role of
bureaucracy, on the importance of resisting individuals or groups
and on the strategy of growth.

These studies are being conducted on an ever more empirical
basis, under the impulse of the various necessities and marked
differences in the societies in which the growth action is taking
place or is being planned.

Thus, we have come to a revision of the theory of economic
development for reasons which are seemingly external but, substantially, of an internal order. The classical picture has not
proved to be adequate to embrace a theory of economic expansion just as the capitalistic economy has not proved to be
historically capable of expanding beyond the originally industrialized countries.[18] We could, thus, find a sort of historical
justification for the first series of reasons; but for the second,
the reasons are actual and pressing; economy has been changing, through a radical evolution, from economy of want to economy of wealth; this is the radically new fact since World War II.

Economic science, which progressively changed into the science of economic expansion, has finalized its contribution to the

[17] Cf. "Les résistances aux changements," in *Revue Internationale des Sciences Sociales,* XII, 3 (1960), pp. 533-41.
[18] Cf. the work by P. Saraceno mentioned before.

maintenance and increase of the rate of income and has faithfully accepted the myth of production. This finalization, accepted as *obvious,* has been brought to a state of crisis by the very manner in which the process of formation of a wealthy society has taken place. The economic theory, in fact, had taken its start from the examination of the producers' and consumers' behavior in an environmental scarcity of material goods. Thus it had focused its attention on the problems related to the maximum increment of production and to satisfying the need for goods by means of production.

The situation, however, with the passing of time, has changed. The capability of the systems of industrialized countries to insure (under markedly economical conditions coupled with high and steadily increasing levels of income and consumption) the full employment of productive factors and resources, has sidetracked the problems of production and consumption which are, to an ever-increasing degree, entrusted to technicians who are experts in production and marketing. The science of organization has prevailed over that of need.

Meanwhile one has become aware of the rise, within the same economic framework, of new forces, motivations, elements, the evaluation of which was, strictly speaking, not within the domain of economic analysis, nor of the new technocratic methods. The evermore extended and intensified action of public enterprise along with integrated private units; the very type of the market's growth characterized by production structures that were at times markedly different from those of free competition; the reduction of the atomism of the decisions with respect to supply as well as to demand; the ever-mounting evidence, within industrialized countries, of requirements and needs that were either inadequately answered or (even if still in a latent stage) could not be considered less pressing; all this has posed economic questions whose solution cannot depend on a criterion based on *economic theory itself,* and, least of all, on one of *efficiency.*

Consumption always seems to be more of an independent social variable rather than a function of production. From Smith to Ricardo, from Malthus to Marx the admission of a general and progressive want had been the premise of economic science, hence the production of goods and of wealth (by means of maximizing the capital and of reaching a rate of growth to guarantee it) had been the imperative condition.

In modern economy (which has become wealth economy) the most urgent need is that of laying down regulations to govern expansion; but these regulations are not meant to control the rate of increment (held to be positive and insured by an evermore self-propelling system)[19] but, rather, the redistribution of investments. The key problem is no longer that of redistributing existing wealth—the classical problem of equality—but rather that of devolving the maximum disposable share of yielded income increase so as to transform the accumulation of capital in relation to the public interest. This is intended to modify the living and working conditions of all members of the community (first of all the depressed ones) in order to insure security and a new social equilibrium. The social change then takes place within an economic structure that rejects the traditional schemes. Wealth is being conceived otherwise; to rest on the myth of production of consumer goods is no longer possible. The growth conception is therefore radically changed, and this becomes more evident if we look at the transposition of this contrast of modern societies, that produces even more ambiguities in backward countries.

Should a world still in search of itself and also lacking that thrust, which is the characteristic of modern technology, be confronted with the same dilemma characterizing the modern and wealthy economy? The latter is struggling more and more between the myth of production of consumer goods and social equilibrium, which is attained by shouldering an ever-growing load of social and civic responsibilities aimed at taking account of individual and social capital which, most times, cannot be "quantified". Certainly the nature of the incentives, the remuneration for work—which generate different behavior or reactions in relation to the mentality and expectations of the individuals

[19] Cf. the work by P. Saraceno, *L'Italia verso la piena occupazione* (Milan, 1963).

and of the more or less organized groups—cannot be applied in underdeveloped zones on the basis of factors evaluated in a mental and economic framework that is accepted only inasmuch as it is "modern". One should, instead, investigate every single reality with objectivity and a spirit of participation in order to work out plans of action and to correct, if necessary, the same perspectives drawn from other experiences.

At this point, actually, one could conclude that all most recent studies are slowly leading to a thorough revision of the traditional conception of economic expansion and are offering contributions toward the definition of a new content. The ecoomic growth-process, therefore, cannot be considered except as a process of transformation of the whole society in which not only determinate sectional aspects are involved but society itself, taken as a complex and historically formed organism. Economic transformation, thus, is a determining factor in promotion of the growth-process. However, it is not the only factor responsible for growth since the latter is to be considered as an organic and orderly (even if not simultaneous) transformation of the economic structure, of the social structure, of cultural aims and attitudes, of the administrative organization, of juridical institutions and so on. Side by side with economic transformations, social, cultural, juridical and administrative changes should take place since they are the only ones that concur to promote a firm hold in the single underdeveloped realities.

Such a position, obviously, cannot exclude the even more fundamental theme: that end toward which society leads or is led, and for which the adoption of adequate measures is politically justified and pursued. The effort to define is an almost daily task in the world reality of today, and it is prompted by an ever-expanding policy of planning and programming.

It is already evident, however, that the vision of economic growth implying organic expansion toward the ideal has proved to be correct in the light of the historical experience of these past years. And this further lessens the time during which the Church will find and perform her role.

# PART IV

CHRONICLE OF THE
LIVING CHURCH

# Introduction

I t might be possible to let this section, the final contribution to each volume, serve as a brief relaxation after pages of deep theological thought—a kind of "Bar Jonah" (the Council coffee bar) where tired readers, like the Council Fathers, can enjoy a break. Unfortunately, this cannot be; it would only add to the popular impression that theology is something separate from the ordinary round of daily life.

Theology follows the Church's life in every sense. It follows in the sense of "accompanying with loving attention" and of "reflecting in the presence of". It also follows in the sense of "coming after"—to think or reflect after the fact, to conclude, to complete. Insofar as it reflects upon the life of the Church, it both depends on this life and helps to give it direction. All this would hardly provoke queries or opposition, were not theology also involved in the complex phenomenon which we might designate as lack of communication or limited communication in the Church. On the one hand, theology is the most "committed" science (Karl Rahner); on the other hand, it is in fact, though not in principle, exposed to the danger of plying its trade outside the human tumult and of failing, finally, to enter the rushing mainstream of the Church's life. This produces an estrangement which appears today as defeatism among some theologians and preachers, and as complaints by the ordinary faithful who feel excluded from the world of those same theologians and preachers because of the totally different and separate language.

Without wishing to oversimplify the distinction between the "reflective" and the "pre-reflective" elements in the Church's life, but rather, fully aware of how closely interwoven these elements are, we must say that in some aspects the living Church shows traces of theological and scientific reflection. Such reflection, once planted in the Church's life, begins to bear fruit in living practice, in institutional problems, pastoral planning and experiments. In other aspects, however, the living Church is still in the pre-reflective state: not yet shaped into a clear theological theme, not yet the subject of theological reflection, but showing aspects of reality that perhaps diverge from current theological reflection, or have fallen behind, or, on the contrary, lie ahead of the present state of reflection and for that reason can and must stimulate further reflection.

Realities in the Church's life that, either in their concrete aspect or in their divergent contemporary character and meaning, have not yet become the subject of theological reflection, may already have become the subject of responsible scientific study. Today, more than ever before, the Church's life is being explored with the aid of exact sciences (application of statistics to quantitative data), or with the help of the Arts (in the academic sense) and phenomenology (the descriptive analysis of concrete existence), or by a happy combination of these approaches, or, in a more passing fashion, by excellent journalistic reporting. It is studied, with or without specific theological contributions, in conferences, days of study, general meetings and a variety of publications.

Guided by this rapidly increasing material, a professional theologian or anyone interested in theology should be able to obtain a sound idea of, for example, the meaning of Sunday in the life of contemporary man in Western Europe; or, again by way of example, the impact upon the faithful of the Sunday sermon. Again, some particular research project might bring to light what tendencies, in what measure and in what connection, prevail among certain sectors of the Church community in the matter of marital morality, different perhaps from current opinions in theological textbooks but nonetheless valuable for both theology and the theologian.

This section is therefore intended to report on such material, not always accessible to everyone perhaps, because one or other important piece of research has failed to attract attention outside its group or country of origin. This type of material, moreover, is frequently presented in language that must be made clearer and more precise for the uninitiated. Finally and above all, this material is so vast and is made public in so many different ways that one can only keep up with it, ordinarily, by constant attention to many surveys and summaries.

It is not our intention to compete with the daily press, radio or television in "hot news" or "scoops". This section merely wishes to draw the attention of theologians and those interested in theology to contributions on topical aspects of the living Church, or, if you like, to provide "flashes" to light up a contemporary "biography" of the living Church, to act as distress signals, or reconnaissance symbols, or beacons or simply as hopeful and encouraging signs.

# The International Congress on Education for the Priesthood in Western Europe

An International Congress on education for the priesthood in Western European seminaries was held (August 31-September 3) at the Europa-Seminarie, Rothem-Meerssen, Netherlands under the chairmanship of Most Rev. Franz Jachym, Archbishop-Coadjutor of Vienna, with Msgr. J. Dellepoort, Director of the Institute for Assistance to Priests in Europe as vice-chairman. Guided by the report on this Congress (soon to be published in French and German by the Instituut voor Europese Priesterhulp, Stokstraat 53, Maastricht, Netherlands), we wish briefly in this article to indicate some of the subjects treated there, with reference to various addresses given at the Congress, by way of introduction to the resolutions which have in the meantime been passed on to the Conciliar Commission for seminary training, and which we shall reproduce here unabridged.

## The Present Situation

A clear picture of training for the priesthood in Western European seminaries was given in the reports drafted by, among others, Linus Grond, O.F.M. (Weert, Netherlands), Raymond Izard (Director of the Centre National Français des Vocations, Paris) and Joseph Möller (Tübingen, West Germany). In a very general way one can distinguish two main streams: the French type, characteristic of 81 out of the 87 French seminaries (the five exceptions are the university seminaries of Paris, Lille, Toulouse, Angers and Lyons, and also the seminary of the Mission de France at Pontigny), which served as model for the seminaries of Belgium and Holland; the German type, which is broadly followed in Switzerland and Austria.

The foundation for the French type was laid in 1651 by M. Olier, parish priest of Saint-Sulpice in Paris. Even today the French method is still dominated by the Société de St. Sulpice, emphasizing spiritual formation, severe discipline and a rather closed-in atmosphere which makes seminarians appreciate the more their eighteen-months' military service without privileges, etc. The seeds for a new development lie in the typically Sulpician emphasis on individual spiritual direction. A start has also been made with the formation of teams that prepare the liturgy of the mass collectively and with the practice of spiritual dialogue and "revision de vie". The teams are appointed by the authority; initiatives, too, come from the authority, and the teams have no share in the responsibility for the affairs of their seminary.

In the German type, seminarians of most German dioceses follow courses at a university or Catholic faculty so that the seminary is only a hostel for them. The diocese designates a university where the candidate for the priesthood can study philosophy and a large part of his theology. There is also the custom of leaving the student free to choose his university for the first year of theology. All German theological faculties adjust their program accordingly (the so-called *Freies Jahr*), and so do Innsbruck, Austria and Fribourg, Switzerland. After eight years the seminarians leave the university and spend the last one-and-a-half or two years in the *Priesterseminar*. In Germany higher demands are generally made on the intellectual ability of the candidates, and before they enter they must possess a certificate of secondary education, recognized by the State.

## *"Aggiornamento" of Training for the Priesthood*

Gradually, and at different paces, the conviction has grown that seminary training is not sufficiently adjusted to the present situation in Church and world. There are important changes taking place insofar as the candidates themselves are concerned: an increasing number of vocations come from the working classes; several seminaries have already decided to accept candidates who have had no classical or academic education; late vocations, in particular, have increased (in some countries by 20%), and these come largely from the world of technology. New approaches are, therefore, indicated, and the Congress underlined the need for an introductory seminary period as well as for a period, before or after ordination, of preparation for pastoral practice.

Another cause which presses for an *aggiornamento* of training for the priesthood is the importance attached today to the human person, his conscience and his responsibility. As Most Rev. Reuss, Auxiliary Bishop of Mainz, West Germany, put it: "It would be a very poor system of education which would try to make candidates for the priesthood conform to a standard formula without taking into account their personality. One single norm is essential: disposition and behavior must conform to Jesus Christ. The candidate himself can only approach this norm by a slow growth on the lines of his own individuality, with his faults and shortcomings and with the help of God's grace. Candidates with a strong personality are without doubt a true cross for their educators, but this cross, precisely insofar as it is a cross, is a gift of God. Priest-educators must not yield to the temptation to escape from that cross by trying to make all seminarians conform to one pattern and by eliminating those who cannot be forced into that one pattern."

The most urgent reason for this *aggiornamento*—which is part of the *aggiornamento* of the whole Church—lies in the rapid change which has affected the priestly image. This point was put to the Congress by Walter Goddijn, O.F.M. (Rotterdam, Netherlands) and Paul Anciaux (President of the Seminary of Malines, Belgium). Large groups among the faithful and many seminarians, too, are struggling with an antiquated priestly image which is influenced by an out-of-date phase in the relationship between the Church and the world; during that period the priest had not only a religious and sacred function, but was also frequently social leader and emancipator.

In our day the priest must face a many-sided conflict as to what parts he is supposed to play. In the present relationship between Church and world the priestly image is frequently obscured for both priests and faithful, and has created a serious problem, either as a whole or in one of its aspects (*e.g.,* the connection of priesthood and celibacy). All this has consequences, not only with regard to seminary training, but also, as is more and more emphasized today, with regard to all that is implied in that for later development: the pastoral support of priests, after their studies, in their human and spiritual growth and in the discharge of their task. But this also prompts the question as to whether a special training of the teachers should not receive more and systematic treatment.

*Resolutions Passed by the Congress*

1. The second Congress has dealt with the formation of students for the priesthood in various countries of Western Europe. To start with, it has noted that there exists a fair amount of converging investigations that already lead to certain common conclusions. These derive mainly from the fact that the rapid development now taking place in Church and world, and in their mutual relationship, demands a new priestly image. This implies that training for the priesthood must take account of the demands

implied in this image-to-be, and must attempt a deeper theology of the priesthood.

Therefore the Congress considers it necessary to multiply the efforts required by this adjustment. It is also convinced that priestly training in the seminary must be complemented by continuous and additional training after the seminary period.

2. The problems that have arisen in the way indicated above deserve thorough investigation in the opinion of this Congress. For this reason the Congress invites the Institute for Assistance to Priests in Europe to set up a special international study commission, composed of theologians, sociologists and psychologists (clerical and lay). The terms of reference for this commission would be to study the following questions: the function of the priest in the modern world; the consequences of this for the scientific, spiritual and pastoral formation of the priest; the problem of celibacy (particularly its foundation with its anthropological and religious presuppositions); the formation of those in charge of priestly training; and finally, the new relationship between bishops and priests, and between priests and laity, keeping in mind the democratization of the modern way of life on every level. The Congress also recommends the setting up of similar commissions by the appropriate ecclesiastical authorities in the participating countries.

3. The Congress expresses the desire that in the training for the priesthood the genuine freedom of the candidates in the choice of their vocation be guaranteed, together with the greatest opportunity for their maturing as men, Christians and priests. Consequently, the Congress recommends a revision of the training where this may seem necessary. The Congress also expresses the wish that bishops be granted complete freedom by the Council to take the necessary steps toward this end, such as the introduction of probationary tasks before ordination or the search for ways and means to do more justice to the candidates' individuality during their training. As a consequence of this, the Congress hopes that the Council will accept the suitability of postponing ordination to a riper age.

4. The Congress recommends that the training start with a special introductory course to prepare candidates more intensively for priestly spirituality, the studies that are to follow and the future fulfillment of their function. In this course special emphasis should be put on the priestly realization of poverty according to Christ's example.

5. The Congress also suggests that priests, already engaged in the ministry, be given more help in the development of their spiritual life according to the successive phases of their life. Their pastoral activity should also be accompanied by further formation.

6. The Congress requests that theologians study more deeply the theological background of the priestly function and the collegiality of priests.

7. The Congress recommends the implementation of a life of apostolic and spiritual collegiality in the seminary, *e.g.,* by the formation of smaller groups (*équipes,* teams). This would prepare candidates for the social structures within which they have to live and work.

8. The Congress expresses the desire that there be room in the training for a more intensive contact with the laity and Christian households.

9. The Congress wonders whether more recognition should not be given to a wider individual differentiation in view of modern pastoral work, the unfolding of the seminarians' own personalities and the difference in their individual growth.

10. The Congress requests the Institute for Assistance to Priests in Europe to develop international documentation on the problems concerning the priesthood and priestly training and to organize an information service for this purpose for specialists in the participating countries.

11. The Congress expresses the wish that the findings of the above mentioned study commission be presented to the next Congress to be convened as soon as the commission has finished its task, in any case before Easter 1967.

International Publishers of CONCILIUM

ENGLISH EDITION
Paulist Press
*Glen Rock, N. J., U.S.A.*
Burns & Oates Ltd.
25 Ashley Place
London, S.W.1

DUTCH EDITION
Uitgeverij Paul Brand, N.V.
*Hilversum, Netherlands*

FRENCH EDITION
Maison Mame
*Tours/Paris, France*

GERMAN EDITION
Verlagsanstalt Benziger & Co., A.G.
*Einsiedeln, Switzerland*
Matthias Grunewald-Verlag
*Mainz, W. Germany*

SPANISH EDITION
Ediciones Guadarrama
*Madrid, Spain*

PORTUGUESE EDITION
Livraria Morais Editora, Ltda.
*Lisbon, Portugal*